FROM LANCASTER ᴛᴏ THE LAKES: THE REGION IN LITERATURE

Six essays by

David Craig, Keith Hanley, Alison Milbank,
Helen Phillips and David Steel

Centre for North-West Regional Studies
University of Lancaster

1992

General Editor: Oliver M. Westall

This volume is the twenty-fourth in a series published by the Centre for North-West Regional Studies at the University of Lancaster. Details of other titles in the series which are available may be found at the back of this volume.

ISSN 0308–4310

Published by the Centre for North-West Regional Studies, University of Lancaster

Typeset in 10/12 Times by Carnegie Publishing Ltd., Maynard Street, Preston
Printed and bound in the UK by The Bath Press, Bath

First Edition, 1992

British Library Cataloguing-in-Publication Data
A CIP catalogue record for this book is available from the British Library

ISBN 0-901800-03-1

Table of Contents

List of Figures iv

Acknowledgements. vi

Preface vii

1   Wordsworth's 'Region of the Peaceful Self'
Keith Hanley 1

2   Coming Home:
the Romantic Tradition of Mountaineering
David Craig 27

3   Charles Dickens, John Ruskin and the old King's Arms
Royal Hotel, Lancaster, with Seven Letters to its
Landlord Mr. Joseph Sly
David Steel 41

4   Mrs Humphry Ward and the Great Houses of
Westmorland: Levens Hall and Sizergh Castle
Alison Milbank. 59

5   Ruskin's Views:
Gloom and Glory in Kirkby Lonsdale
Keith Hanley 72

6   'Arts and Kindliness':
Gordon Bottomley and his Circle
Helen Phillips 94

Contributors. 111

List of Figures

1.1   Joseph Wilkinson, *Coniston Water-head*, from his *Select Views in Cumberland, Westmorland, and Lancashire*, 1810. 4

1.2   T. H. Fielding and, *Esthwaite Water*, from *A Picturesque Tour of the English Lakes*, 1821. 7

1.3   William Gilpin, *Furness Abbey*, from his *Northern Tour*, 1786. 9

1.4   J. M. W. Turner, *Lancaster Sands*, c.1825.
Reproduced with the permission of the Department of Prints and Drawings of the British Museum. 13

1.5   Sir George Beaumont, *Peele Castle*, 1806.
Private collection; reproduced with the owner's permission. 16

1.6   Joseph Farington, *South View of Lancaster*, from his *The Lakes of Lancashire, Westmorland, and Cumberland*, 1816. 20

1.7   J. M. W. Turner, *The Gateway at Lancaster Castle*, from his *Views in Lancashire and Yorkshire, from original drawings*, 1872. 22

1.8   'Hanging' chair, Lancaster Castle.
Reproduced with the permission of the *Westmorland Gazette*. 23

2.1   Thomas Gainsborough, *Romantic Landscape with Sheep at a Spring*, 1783.
Reproduced with the permission of the Royal Academy of Arts. 28

2.2   David Craig and Bill Peascod on Dexter Wall, Grey Crag, Birkness, June 1982.
Photograph by Chris Culshaw. 37

2.3   David Craig and Bill Peascod on 'Haste Not', White Gill, Great Langdale, August 1983.
Photograph by Chris Culshaw. 38

3.1   The Old King's Arms Hotel, Lancaster, May 1879.
Reproduced with the permission of Lancaster City Museum and Art Gallery. . . . 48

3.2   Entrance Hall and Ancient Staircase, King's Arms Hotel, Lancaster.
Reproduced with the permission of Lancaster City Museum and Art Gallery. . . . 49

3.3   R. J. Lane, Lithograph of Charles Dickens.
Reproduced with the permission of Lancaster City Museum and Art Gallery. . . . 52

4.1   Max Beerbohm, from his *The Poet's Corner*, 1904. 60

4.2   Thomas Allom, *Interior of Sizergh Hall, Westmorland*, from his
      *Picturesque Rambles in Westmorland, Cumberland, Durham and
      Northumberland*, 1847. 62

4.3   Thomas Allom, *Levins Hall, Westmorland*, from his *Picturesque
      Rambles in Westmorland, Cumberland, Durham and
      Northumberland*, 1847. 63

4.4   Window from the old church, Cartmel Fell.
      Photograph by Alison Milbank. 70

5.1   J. M. W. Turner, *Heysham and Cumberland Mountains*, 1818.
      Reproduced with the permission of the Department of Prints and Drawings of
      the British Museum. 73

5.2   J. M. W. Turner, *Crook of Lune, looking towards Hornby Castle*,
      1817–18.
      Reproduced with the permission of the Courtauld Institute Galleries. 74

5.3   J. M. W. Turner, *Kirkby Lonsdale Churchyard*, 1817–18.
      Private collection; reproduced with the owner's permission. 76

5.4   John Ruskin, engraving of J. M. W. Turner's *Egglestone Abbey*, from
      the Library Edition of *The Works of John Ruskin*, ed. E. T. Cook
      and Alexander Wedderburn, 1903–12. 77

5.5   The Crystal Palace, from the *Art Journal Catalogue*, 1851. 84

5.6   Terra cotta ornamentation of the British History Museum, from *The
      Builder*, 1878. 85

5.7   John Ruskin, engraving of a detail from J. M. W. Turner's *Garden of
      the Hesperides*, from *Modern Painters*, volume 5, 1860. 86

5.8   John Ruskin, *Seascale Sands*, 1889.
      Reproduced with the permission of The Ruskin Galleries, Bembridge School. . . . 91

6.1   William Rothenstein, Portrait of Gordon Bottomley, 1922.
      Reproduced with the permission of Tullie House, Carlyle Art Gallery and
      Museum. 95

6.2   Paul Nash, *Foliage*, 1914.
      Reproduced with the permission of The Paul Nash Trust. 101

6.3   Paul Nash, *The Monkey Tree*, 1914.
      Reproduced with the permission of The Paul Nash Trust. 102

Acknowledgements

'Wordsworth's "Region of the Peaceful Self" ' is a version of a paper given to the Wordsworth Seminar on 'Literature, Culture, and Region' at Lancaster University in 1992, and was based on lectures delivered for the Adult Continuing Education Department of Lancaster University at the Duke's Playhouse, Lancaster, in 1983, for Newcastle University's Centre for Continuing Education at the Brewery Arts Centre, Kendal, in 1989, and for the Blue Badge Guides at Charlotte Mason College, Ambleside, in 1990. 'Ruskin's Views: Gloom and Glory in Kirkby Lonsdale' is a version of a paper given to the Ruskin Seminar, Lancaster University, 1992. 'Coming Home: the Romantic Tradition of Mountaineering' is a version of a chapter in David Craig's *Native Stones* (Secker and Warburg, 1987), and appears here with the copyright-holder's permission.

We are grateful for the following permissions to reproduce: to the Department of Prints and Drawings of the British Museum for Turner's *Lancaster Sands* and *Heysham and Cumberland Mountains*; to the Royal Academy of Arts for Gainsborough's *Romantic Landscape with Sheep at a Spring*; to the Courtauld Institute Galleries for Turner's *Crook of Lune, Looking towards Hornby Castle*; to the private owners of Beaumont's *Peele Castle* and Turner's *Kirkby Lonsdale Churchyard*; to the Ruskin Galleries, Bembridge School, for Ruskin's drawing *Seascale Sands*; to Tullie House, Carlyle Art Gallery and Museum, for William Rothenstein's portrait of Gordon Bottomley; to Chris Culshaw for the climbing photographs in chapter two; to Lancaster City Museum and Art Gallery for the photographs in chapter three; to Alison Milbank for the photograph in chapter four; to the *Westmorland Gazette* for the photograph of the 'Hanging' chair; and to the Paul Nash Trust for the Nash paintings in chapter six.

Every effort has been made to contact the copyright holders in order to obtain permission to reprint. If any copyright holder has been overlooked the publisher will be pleased to print an acknowledgement in any subsequent edition of this work.

Preface

These essays discuss the works of several writers who were directly influenced by their experience of a particular area in the North-West of England: from Lancaster to the Lakes. The terrain that they cover is difficult to map precisely, as it overlaps from North Lancashire into the Lake District counties and North Yorkshire; but this geographical indeterminacy only serves to increase the sense of cultural marginality that attaches to it and that has made it a ready site for cultural displacements.

The area that has featured in a series of novels, poems, plays, and other writings is an intermediate one. On the fringes of the Lakes, it is located between the metropolitan centres of London in the south and Edinburgh in the north. During the period when Wordsworth and Coleridge, Ruskin, Dickens, Mary Ward and Gordon Bottomley were writing – from the late eighteenth to the early twentieth centuries – it was a borderland between new and old, between the separate regions of industrial Lancashire and the Romantic heartland of the Lakes. For Wordsworth and Ruskin it was the territory on which major cultural shifts were negotiated between the sacred, represented in the picturesque beauty of the Lakes and the Lune valley, and a new spirit of nationalism and commercial imperialism. For others, however, its attraction was that in some way it seemed time had largely passed it by, so that for them it was most firmly placed in an alternative history. For Mary Ward, for example, it was the redoubt of the old Catholic north; for Dickens it was a curiously ancient province. For Bottomley, it was a transitional space, where traditional ruralism could mute the shock of modernism, without cancelling innovation. Further into the Lakes, for Coleridge and those Romantic mountaineers whom he influenced, it had offered a strangely familiar encounter with an other and ultimate self, on the edge between life and death.

We have included many photographs and illustrations because, in such a moot landscape, buildings and scenes take on symbolic importance as monuments, retreats or landmarks by which to take cultural and historical bearings. Specific locations, such as Levens Hall and Sizergh Castle, or the old King's Arms Royal Hotel in Lancaster, or the face of 'Haste Not' in Great Langdale, or a view from Bottomley's house in Silverdale, become focuses of particular meanings, and, sometimes, as with Wordsworth's Furness Abbey, Piel and Lancaster Castles, and Ruskin's view from Kirkby Lonsdale Churchyard, they are even seen to stand at the centre of the nation.

K. H. and A. M.
The Wordsworth Centre

Chapter One

Wordsworth's 'Region of the Peaceful Self'

Keith Hanley

In 1817 an article in the *Edinburgh Review* referred disparagingly to what it identified as the 'Lake school' of writers.[1] The piece was chiefly about a book by Samuel Taylor Coleridge, who first took his family to Greta Hall, Keswick, in 1800 and made it his chief residence until his exile to Malta in 1804; but the association was more particularly appropriate for William Wordsworth than for either Coleridge or for the other writers involved – the Poet Laureate, Robert Southey, who had also gone to live at Greta Hall in 1803, and stayed there until his death in 1843, and later Thomas De Quincey, who settled in Grasmere in 1809 and finally left Westmorland in 1828. Not only was Wordsworth born and bred in the Lake District (living there for all but twelve of his eighty years), but his poetry, in literal and more indirect ways, is steeped in his experience of that region more than any other writer's work.

It may be surprising, however, to realise how much of his most memorable poetry is in fact set completely *outside* the Lake District. His first great poem, 'The Ruined Cottage' (composed 1797–8), which tells the heart-rending story of a deserted mother's slow decline and the ruin of the family home, is placed in the landscape of the West Country. In what is generally regarded as his masterpiece, the long autobiographical poem, *The Prelude*, which he wrote in its first complete form in 1805,[2] the twin climaxes, when the poet sees his imagination mirrored in panoramic views of nature, describe his travelling over the Simplon Pass in Switzerland (VI, 549–72) and the view gained from an ascent of Mount Snowdon by night (XIII, 10–119). The central metaphor for the creative power of the imagination in that poem:

> The senseless mass,
> In its projections, wrinkles, cavities,
> Through all its surface, with all colours streaming,
> Like a magician's airy pageant, parts,
> Unites, embodying everywhere some pressure
> Or image, recognised or new, some type
> Or picture of the world (VIII, 731–7)

is based on the mysterious interior of the cave of the Norse giant, Yordas, near Ingleton in North Yorkshire, and other well-known works were composed, for example, 'a few miles above Tintern Abbey, on revisiting the banks of the Wye' in 1798, and 'upon Westminster Bridge' in 1802.

Yet all these poems, (and arguably every other poem by Wordsworth), are informed by the same perception of an underlying structure of unity in both nature and the human mind. The mind either sees or creates this oneness which, once established, in turn composes and consoles the troubled mind. This power – Wordsworth's imagination – was formed by the peace and security he had experienced from early childhood in the inland vales of the Lake District, and from the deep sense of harmony which responded to that scenery a conviction of the moral order in the universe was gradually to evolve. Because this structure had originated in relation to places and buildings in the Lake District, wherever else Wordsworth went and whenever he turned his attention to national or international events, he never left those scenes entirely behind. But in organising the bearing of the Lakes on the world outside, the southern fringes of the district took on a particular importance.

(1)

Tracing the origins of Wordsworth's imagination leads us to focus on the *Lancashire Wordsworth* – a connection that De Quincey writes, in the revised edition of *Confessions of an English Opium-Eater* (1856), he was eager to make when he was growing up in Manchester:

> The southern region of that district, about eighteen or twenty miles long, which bears the name of Furness, figures in the eccentric geography of English law as a section of Lancashire, though separated from that county by the estuary of Morecambe Bay: and therefore, as Lancashire happened to be in my own native county, I had from childhood, on the strength of this mere legal fiction, cherished as a mystic privilege, slender as a filament of air, some fraction of Denizenship in the fairy little domain of the English Lakes.[3]

The passage has a resonance for all those who like to avail themselves of a culturally privileged version of their northernness. Though most of the Lake District lay in what was then Westmorland and Cumberland, in order to claim his preferred ground, De Quincey separates out the area of North Lancashire – Lonsdale North of the Sands, and particularly High and Low Furness – which had been crucially formative for Wordsworth:

> the sweet reposing little water of Esthwaite, with its few emerald fields, and the grander one of Coniston, with the sublime cluster of mountain groups, and the little network of dells lurking about its head all the way back to Grasmere . . . together with the ruins of the once glorious (Furness) abbey (*Works*, I, 74).

Before the completion of the Furness Railway in 1846, the protracted entrance into the region was by coach to Lancaster, then to Hest Bank, and across the Sands at low tide. The territory of Furness and Cartmel was on the margin of the Lake District, part of the transitional coastal area between region and nation. While it was in touch with constant traffic from an outer world, most immediately from what was becoming the industrial heartland of South Lancashire, it was also hemmed in and cut off by the curving bay. It was an actual border location, between a familiar everyday world and intimations of something glimpsed beyond which is the keynote of Wordsworth's imaginative vision.[4]

Throughout their lives, the Wordsworth family had faith in the therapeutic effects of the sea-air around their most immediate coastline.[5] In 1811, Wordsworth and his wife took their children, Thomas and Catharine, for a month to the sea-side near Bootle, where they lived 'under [the] shadow'[6] of Black Comb, the mountain just north of the Duddon Sands, 'at the southern extremity of Cumberland'. (*PW*, II, 289) Two years later, he wrote a poem, 'View From the Top of Black Comb', which evokes the commanding prospect, radiating out from what, in the first version of his *Guide to the Lakes* (1810), he referred to as the 'rim' of the 'imaginary wheel',[7] made up by the eight valleys that spread out from a central point in the Lake District:

> from the summit of BLACK COMB . . .
>   . . . the amplest range
> Of unobstructed prospect may be seen
> That British ground commands: – low dusky tracts,
> Where Trent is nursed, far southward! Cambrian hills
> To the south-west, a multitudinous show;
> And, in a line of eyesight linked with these,
> The hoary peaks of Scotland
>   . . .
>   Of Nature's works,
> In earth, and air, and earth-embracing sea,
> A revelation infinite it seems;
> Display august of man's inheritance,
> Of Britain's calm felicity and power!
> (11.2–9, 30–4; *PW*, II, 289–90)

The mountain on the frontier, between region and nation, provides the point from which the stability of Lakes culture may be seen to be the basis of a potentially world-wide order.

This view of the Lakes had a pedigree. De Quincey alludes to Ann Radcliffe's account of the Lakes (1794) in *A Journey . . . through Holland and the Western Frontier of Germany . . . to which are added Observations during a tour to the Lakes of Lancashire, Westmoreland and Cumberland* (1795), which had popularised Furness in particular, and

> the landscape painters, so many and so various, (who had) contributed to the glorification
> of the English lake district; drawing out and impressing upon the heart the sanctity of
> repose in its shy recesses – its Alpine grandeurs in such passes as those of Wastdale-head,
> Langdale-head, Borrowdale, Kirkstone, Hawsdale, &c., together with the monastic peace
> which seems to brood over its peculiar form of pastoral life (*Works*, I, 74–5).

As has been pointed out, 'interest in the north-west had been roused in the Jacobite Rebellion of 1745.'[8] In the second half of the eighteenth century, improved roads and increased interest in landscape art, especially as reproduced in engravings, led to a spate of published *Tours*. The artists preceded the writers: William Bellers published his print, 'A View of Derwent-Water towards Borrowdale. A Lake near Keswick' in 1752, and Thomas Smith three prints in 1761. Dr. John Brown's pamphlet, *A Description of the lake at Keswick, (and the adjacent country) in Cumberland* (published five times between 1767 and 1772), was the first work devoted specifically to this area, and the first guide-book was Thomas West's *A Guide to the Lakes: Dedicated to the Lovers of*

Landscape Studies, and to all who have Visited, or Intend to Visit the Lakes in Cumberland, Westmorland and Lancashire (seven editions between 1778 and 1800). Gray's journal of his Lakes tour made in 1769 which offers a series of sensitively personal observations was published in 1775, but the most influential successor to West's book, complete with engraved aquetint plates, was *Observations, Relative Chiefly to Picturesque Beauty, Made in the Year 1772, on Several Parts of England, Particularly the Mountains, and Lakes of Cumberland and Westmoreland* (1786) by William Gilpin, (the original of the 'Dr. Syntax' satires on the cult of the picturesque), who combined the roles of artist and guide. The last and most comprehensive of the eighteenth-century works on the Lake District, incorporating selections from almost every author who had written about its history, archaeology and topography, was William Hutchinson's *A History of Cumberland* (1794). Led by these books, upper class southerners began to visit the district as an alternative to the Grand Tour, when the French Revolution closed the continent to English travellers, and, as has been suggested, there was a developing 'element of chauvinism in equating' English artists such as Smith with Claud Lorrain.[9]

West and Gilpin were advocates of the Claude Lorrain glass, a small, dark, convex mirror, in which the tourist was to view the reduced proportions of a landscape scene. Brown had famously remarked that 'the full perfection of *Keswick* consists of three circumstances, Beauty, Horror, and Immensity united',[10] but, especially under the influence of Gilpin's sense of 'picturesque beauty', the emphasis was on unity rather than

Figure 1.1: Joseph Wilkinson, *Coniston Water-head*, from his *Select Views in Cumberland, Westmorland, and Lancashire*, 1810.

contrast. The picturesque approach cultivated the perception of only small-scale contrasts, which, miniaturised in the Claude glass, reflected the dominant civilised values of stability and order for the social class by which they were pleasurably superintended.

The tradition of the picturesque representation of the Lake District, always with a human presence in the foreground, sees nature consistently subdued to social purposes, recreational or working. This was the genre to which Wordsworth contributed in the text he provided to accompany a series of engravings, *Select Views in Cumberland, Westmoreland, and Lancashire* (1810), by the Rev. Joseph Wilkinson. (Figure 1.1) It was a reactionary aesthetic that, as the nation underwent increased stresses from within and without, came to represent in provincial scenes the immemorial bedrock of the British way of life. This was the territory – no longer on the fringes but at the heart of the nation – that Wordsworth later believed he was helping to mediate in the book which in its fifth edition was entitled *A Guide Through the District of the Lakes* (1835). During his lifetime, it was by far his most popular work.

(2)

Above all, 'the deep deep magnet' (*Works*, I, 75) that drew De Quincey to the Lakes was Wordsworth's poetry. At the time about which he is writing, 1801–1802, De Quincey knew only the first two editions of *Lyrical Ballads* (1798, 1800), but he was, apart from Coleridge and Wordsworth's family, the only devotee who was allowed an advance reading of the manuscript of *The Prelude*, (the autobiographical poem first published posthumously in 1850, though completed in separate versions in 1799 and 1805), in which Wordsworth described the great 'spots of time' (XI, 257) from his childhood, when his mind first awoke to its relation with nature.

Several of these spooky episodes occurred in the vale of Esthwaite, while Wordsworth was at Hawkshead Grammar School and living in a joiner's cottage at Colthouse. He went there at the age of nine in 1779, and the fullest detailed account of the place during the eight years he spent there is given by T. W. Thompson.[11] Just after arriving there, Wordsworth had seen a 'heap of garments' (V, 461) on Strickland-ears, a peninsula on Esthwaite, which turned out to be those of a drowned schoolmaster:

> At length, the dead man, 'mid that beauteous scene
> Of trees and hills and water, bolt upright
> Rose with this ghastly face, a spectre shape –
> Of terror even. And yet no vulgar fear,
>
> . . .
>
> Possessed me, for my inner eye had seen
> such sights before among the shining streams
> Of fairyland, the forests of romance –
> Thence came a spirit hallowing what I saw
> With decoration and ideal grace,
> A dignity, a smoothness, like the words
> Of Grecian art and purest poesy. (V, 470–81)

On Keen Ground High and Charity High, the hills behind Hawkshead church,

Wordsworth snared woodcocks by night, and was sometimes tempted to take the birds others had caught. At such times he felt he had offended a retributive moral presence in nature:

> and when the deed was done
> I heard among the solitary hills
> Low breathings coming after me, and sounds
> Of undistinguishable motion, steps
> Almost as silent as the turf they trod. (I, 328–32)

It was a mile and a half north-west of the school, just north of Borwick Ground (or Lodge), that he had an experience that gave rise to a keener sense of 'chastisement' (XI, 369). Just before the Christmas holidays when he was thirteen, he was waiting for the horses his father usually sent to bring him and his brothers home to Cockermouth. When the horses failed to appear, he began to harbour a deep grudge against his father, only to learn subsequently that he was lying mortally ill at the time. His father was dying from the after-effects of exposure, suffered as a result of losing his way in darkness on Cold Fell, just north of Seaton, near Bootle, where, as law-agent and land-steward for Sir James Lowther, he had been conducting two inquests.[12] Later, the scene became associated with recurrent moods of inherited power:

> And afterwards the wind and sleety rain,
> And all the business of the elements,
> The single sheep, and one blasted tree,
> And the bleak music of that old stone wall,
> The noise of wood and water, and the mist
>
>   . . .
>
> All these were spectacles and sounds to which
> I often would repair, and thence would drink
> As at a fountain. And I do not doubt
> That in this later time, when storm and rain
> Beat on my roof at midnight, or by day
> When I am in the woods, unknown to me
> The workings of my spirit thence are brought. (XI, 375–88)

It is, of course, difficult to judge how much Wordsworth's 'memory' has been affected by his intervening history, but what always characterises his temperament and is the concern which occupies all his poetry is the idea of continuity, and avoidance of disruption. Thinking of his birthplace, Cockermouth, and of this 'beloved vale to which erelong/I was transplanted' (I, 308–9), Wordsworth writes that he was 'Fostered alike by beauty and by fear' (I, 306). What seems clear is that his most intense memories of childhood relive a response to nature which, whether directly or after active mental refocusing, represents a deep need to pacify his consciousness of guilt and transgression. In his recollections of the vale of Esthwaite, nature is always framed by the picturesque, which became bolstered by a corresponding sense of moral order to contain whatever stresses his peace of mind came under. (Figure 1.2)

Wordsworth claims that this moral association had already begun to develop when he was fourteen. Fishing trips to the west bank of Coniston were a popular recreation for the schoolboys, and in the 1799 version he writes of the effect on him of 'the radiance of the setting sun . . . reposing on the top/Of the high eastern hills.' (Second Part, 159–61) What he took from the scene was a determination resolutely to look back to – to sustain the memory of – the beautiful scenery that had invested his childhood. The moral structure *was* a matter of being true to that past, a reinforcement of its promise:

> And there I said,
> That beauteous sight before me, there I said
> (Then first beginning in my thoughts to mark
> That sense of dim similitude which links
> Our moral feelings with external forms)
> That in whatever region I should close
> My mortal life I would remember you,
> Fair scenes – that dying I would think on you,
> My soul would send a longing look to you,
> Even as that setting sun. (Second Part, 161–70)

Whether or not Wordsworth had the aesthetic or ethical language to define his experiences exactly in those terms even at that age, up to that point he writes of a more passive education through which 'Nature by extrinsic passion first/Peopled my mind with beauteous forms or grand/And made me love them' (I, 572–4), and describes himself at

Figure 1.2: T. H. Fielding, *Esthwaite Water*, from *A Picturesque Tour of the English Lakes*, 1821.

the age of ten as simply 'drinking in/A pure organic pleasure from the lines/Of curling mist' (I, 590–2). What he identifies in these 'spots' are deep intuitions, the memory of which would *later* help to organise his convictions about art and life. The episode of skating on Esthwaite, in its first version of 1799, ends with an image which coordinates this underlying realisation. He describes how he would suddenly pull himself up short, and how, through his giddiness and the illusion of the continuing motion of the rotating earth, he would gradually assert his greater interest in recovering a more intense perception of the essentially static calm of the physical world in which he lived and moved:

> then at once
> Have I, reclining back upon my heels
> Stopped short – yet still the solitary cliffs
> Wheeled by me, even as if the earth had rolled
> With visible motion her diurnal round.
> Behind me did they stretch in solemn train,
> Feebler and feebler, and I stood and watched
> Till all was tranquil as a summer sea. (First Part, 179–85)

(3)

The most memorable excursions from the home vale were rides to the ruined Cistercian Abbey of St. Mary at Furness (Figure 1.3), 'anxious for one day at least/To feel the motion of the galloping steed.' (II, 102–3) It was a real adventure, with mock-heroic overtones, involving a degree of unruliness. Twenty miles from Hawkshead, 'too distant far/For any cautious man' (107–8), the boys had to lie about their intentions to the innkeeper from whom they hired the horses. Wordsworth's overall description of the ruin oscillates throughout between an exuberant sense of licence and reverence – a rhythm that is contained by the disciplines of the picturesque and the sacred established in his opening passage:

> a mouldering pile with fractured arch,
> Belfry, and images, and living trees –
> A holy scene . . .
> To more than inland peace
> Left by the sea-wind passing overhead
> (Though wind of roughest temper) trees and towers
> May in that valley oftentimes be seen
> Both silent and both motionless alike,
> Such is the shelter that is there, and such
> The safeguard for repose and quietness. (112–21)

But the following passage returns to the sense of escapade:

> Our steeds remounted, and the summons given,
> With ship and spur we by the chauntry flew
> In uncouth race, and left the crossed-legged knight,

8

Figure 1.3: William Gilpin, *Furness Abbey*, from his *Northern Tour*, 1786.

And the stone abbot . . .

> . . .
> Through the walls we flew
> And down the valley, and, a circuit made
> In wantonness of heart, through rough and smooth
> We scampered homeward. (122–5, 135–8)[13]

Yet what makes this episode stand out is its 'joyous' (140) lack of any sense of transgression. There are intimations of suffering, even violation, as the building lies at the mercy of the elements:

> from recent showers
> The earth was comfortless, and, touched by faint
> Internal breezes – sobbings of the place
> And respirations – from the roofless walls
> The shuddering ivy dripped large drops (127–31)

and behind its fall lies a troubled history: what had been the second richest Cistercian abbey in the kingdom surrendered to its dissolution by the Crown in 1537, when the wreckers moved in. Ironically, King Stephen's Foundation Charter for the abbey, 1127, offered it as a counter to the transience and destructiveness, the 'dissolution', of which it was itself to become an image:

> Considering every day the uncertainty of life, that roses and flowers of kings, emperors and dukes, and the crowns and palms of all the great wither and decay: and that all things, with an uninterrupted course, tend to dissolution and death: I therefore return, give, and

grant to God and St. Mary of Furness, all Furness and Walney . . . That in Furness an order of regular monks be by Divine permission established: which gift and offering, I, by supreme authority, appoint to be for ever observed.[14]

In Book VII of *The Excursion* (1814), Wordsworth's poetic persona, the Wanderer, quotes from this charter with his added knowledge that all such historical 'monuments and their memory' (1.999; *PW*, V, 263) are finally reduced to 'nature's pleasant robe of green,/Humanity's appointed shroud' (997–8). For behind this violent history, as behind Wordsworth's own rowdiness, making both finally inoffensive, lies a stronger and unassailable sense of inner pleasure that his relation with nature will never allow to depart:

>   and that single wren
> which one day sang so sweetly in the nave
> Of the old church . . .
>
>   . . .
>
> So sweetly 'mid the gloom the invisible bird
> Sang to itself that there I could have made
> My dwelling-place, and lived for ever there
> To hear such music. (II, 125–7, 132–5)

The result was that in the earliest encounter with the world beyond the confines of his habitual experience – a world that might have been expected to disrupt his untried complaisance and perhaps endorse his own transgressive tendencies – readily gave way to the extension and confirmation of his regulated relation to nature in that world beyond:

>   Oh, ye rocks and streams,
> And that still spirit of the evening air,
> Even in this joyous time I sometimes felt
> Your presence, when, with slackened step, we breathed
> Along the sides of the steep hills, or when,
> Lighted by gleams of moonlight from the sea,
> We beat with thundering hoofs the level sand. (138–44)

(4)

In *The Prelude* Wordsworth described himself in early childhood gazing from the garden behind his father's house at Cockermouth:

> I love a public road: few sights there are
> That please me more – such object hath had power
> O'er my imagination since the dawn
> Of childhood, when its disappearing line
> Seen daily afar off, on one bare steep
> Beyond the limits which my feet had trod,
> Was like a guide to eternity,
> At least to things unknown and without bound. (XII, 145–52)[15]

It was not to be until his mid-twenties that Wordsworth developed any sense of radical difference between the Lakes and what he had seen as their boundless extension into the outer world. *The Prelude* also relates Wordsworth's gradual and then abrupt entry into a world outside the controlling peace and stability of the region. While still a Cambridge undergraduate, he went on a walking tour through France and the Swiss Alps in the summer of 1790, when the French Revolution was one year old. After he returned to France the following year, he became an ardent supporter of the republican cause, was caught up in the disorientating ecstasies of political idealism, and (something which the poem does not refer to), he had a love-affair with a French woman, Annette Vallon, which resulted in the birth of an illegitimate daughter.

Towards the end of 1792 he was forced to return to England, probably from lack of funds. It was a time of great personal frustration and political zeal. In France, the Revolution was taking its course with the execution of Louis XVI in January 1793 of which Wordsworth approved. When, however, the United Kingdom declared war on France in February, Wordsworth experienced the full trauma of 'change and subversion' (X, 233) for the first time:

> No shock
> Given to my moral nature had I known
> Down to that very moment – neither lapse
> Nor turn of sentiment – that might be named
> A revolution, save at this one time. (233–7)

Though during his time in France he had 'bewailed' (IX, 476) the destruction of the sacred picturesque:

> When to a convent in a meadow green
> By a brook-side we came – a roofless pile,
> And not by reverential touch of time
> Dismantled, but by violence abrupt (468–72)

he had seen it as a regrettable consequence of the legitimate crusade for social justice and equality that, despite such horrors as the September Massacres (which he had just missed in Paris on his way back to England), had consistently driven his 'progress on the self-same path/On which with diversity of pace/(He) had been travelling' (X,238–40). Hitherto, he had inhabited an inner 'region of (his) peaceful (self)' (719) that seemed simply to reflect the outer 'very world which is the world/Of all of us' (725–6), but now the declaration had caused him to make 'a stride at once/Into another region.' (241–2)

For Wordsworth, 'a green leaf on the blessed tree/Of my beloved country' (X, 254–5), the Revolution had seemed an organic continuation of a world-order that had always been inherent in his own Lakes culture: 'unto me the events/Seemed nothing out of nature's certain course –/A gift that rather was come late than soon'. (IX, 252–4) Now he had to recognise that William Pitt's national policy ran counter to the provincial convictions of one who '(loved) the sight/Of a village steeple as (he did)' (X, 266–7), as throughout 1793 and 1794 the British government introduced repressive measures and staged treason trials for political thinkers with whom Wordsworth was in sympathy. As a result, he endorsed the just triumphs of the Revolution, even against the British and allied armies, and 'Fed on the day of vengeance yet to come!' (274)

What was even more confusing, however, was that the Revolution needed to be defended from within. In May 1793 the liberal faction of Girondists with whom Wordsworth had associated himself was purged, and in October its leaders were executed. In July Maximilien Robespierre had become president of the Committee of Public Safety, and in September began the Reign of Terror that came to an end only with his fall and execution in July 1794. Wordsworth saw Robespierre as a dictatorial ideologue who was perverting the ideals of the Revolution. He too was to be tested against the original disciplines of North Lancashire.

In August, during this turmoil of allegiances, Wordsworth took a month's recuperative holiday with a cousin at Rampside, on the coast of Furness. (The house he stayed in was the now rebuilt Clarke's Arms Hotel.) Just over three miles inland is Furness Abbey, and one mile from the coast is Piel Castle, on the small island of Foudry, which he refers to in 'Elegiac Stanzas suggested by a Picture of Peele Castle' (1806):

> I was thy neighbour once, thou rugged Pile!
> Four summer weeks I dwelt in sight of thee:
> I saw thee every day; and all the while
> Thy Form was sleeping on a glassy sea.
>
> So pure the sky, so quiet was the air!
> So like, so very like, was day to day! (11.1–6; *PW*, IV, 258–9)

Clearly, it was a scene in which nothing seemed to change – or to have changed. His deepest conviction returned that, as in childhood, 'all was tranquil as a summer sea.'

One morning, in the churchyard of Cartmel priory, he chanced upon the gravestone of his former headmaster at Hawkshead, William Taylor, who had encouraged him to write poetic exercises, and had died during Wordsworth's schooldays. Shortly before dying, Taylor had called the senior boys, including Wordsworth, to his death–bed, telling them 'My head will soon lie low' (X, 501), an expression that may well have recurred strangely to a mind beset with the imagination of mass–guillotining. Invested in the recollection of the melancholic Taylor's early death were strong appeals from that rural Englishness that Wordsworth had been forced to renounce the previous year. Taylor had even requested a fragment of Gray's 'Elegy in a Country Churchyard' to be engraved on his headstone. As Wordsworth returned to Rampside over the estuary of the river Leven, the discovery made him strain backwards, both in memory and by physically turning his gaze, to the region of his unchanging past, congenially clothed in the imagery of a more recent millenarian promise:

> beneath a genial sun,
> With distant prospect among gleams of sky
> And clouds, and intermingled mountain-tops,
> In one inseparable glory clad –
>
>   . . .
>
> Underneath this show
> Lay, as I knew, the nest of pastoral vales
> Among whose happy fields I had grown up
> From childhood. On the fulgent spectacle,
> Which neither changed, nor stirred, nor passed away,

I gazed. (X, 476–9, 483–8)

It was as Wordsworth was crossing the sands (Figure 1.4) that he met

> a variegated crowd
> Of coaches, wains, and travellers, horse and foot,
> Wading, beneath the conduct of their guide,
> In loose procession through the shallow stream
> Of inland water; the great sea meanwhile
> Was at a safe distance, far retired. (524–9)

When Wordsworth asked 'If any news was stirring', he was greeted with the revelation that '*Robespierre was dead*.' (533–5) '[T]he tidings' (537) rushed in on his mind like the tide in Morecambe Bay: with a terrible power from beyond that was, however, controlled by the dominant structure of the picturesque. The scene itself becomes triumphalist, as the reasserted representation of the true revolutionary order – an embattled sacredness – that has conquered over Jacobinism and will insist, when necessary, on the *enforcement* of 'tranquility':

> Great was my glee of spirit, great my joy
> In vengeance, and eternal justice, thus
> Made manifest. 'Come now, ye golden times',

Figure 1.4: J. M. W. Turner, *Lancaster Sands*, c.1825.
Reproduced with the permission of the Department of Prints and Drawings of the British Museum.

13

Said I, forth-breathing on those open sands
A hymn of triumph . . .

             . . .

Then schemes I framed more calmly, when and how
The madding factions might be tranquillized,
And . . .
The mighty renovation would proceed. (X, 539–43, 553–6)

The experience was so crucial for him because it enabled him at last to reconcile his revolutionary idealism with a lasting image of his own national culture. His life had come full circle, as had his boyhood excursions round Furness Abbey. It was that scene, beyond the home vales but, after all, containing the challenge of violence against their lesson of beauty and stability, that had come to prefigure the curbing of revolutionary terrorism:

Thus, interrupted by uneasy bursts
Of exultation, I pursued my way
Along the very shore which I had skimmed
In former times, when, spurring from the Vale
Of Nightshade, and St. Mary's mouldering fane,
And the stone abbot, after circuit made
In wantonness of heart, a joyous crew
Of schoolboys, hastening to their distant home
Along the margin of the moonlight sea,
We beat with thundering hoofs the level sand. (557–66)

By the time Wordsworth came to write this passage in 1805, after he had given himself wholeheartedly to the anti-Napoleonic popular front from 1799, this alternative retrospect on the national culture had become more evidently associated with the more acceptable fact of *British* republicanism, and particularly Milton. As the Norton editors note, the account of this episode is saturated in Miltonic diction. Wordsworth refers to Robespierre's fall in an allusion to *Paradise Lost*

       few happier moments have been mine
Through my whole life than that when first I heard
That this foul tribe of Moloch was o'erthrown,
And their chief regent levelled with the dust. (466–9)

Long after Wordsworth's revolutionary heyday, Hazlitt wrote that Wordsworth's 'Muse' is a 'levelling one',[16] and Wordsworth here had chosen a particularly alienating figure of rebellion *and* kingship – Milton's 'horrid king besmeared with blood/Of human sacrifice, and parents tears',[17] – to represent the conflation of tyranny and revolution, cut down to size when first Robespierre, and then Napoleon had become 'oppressors in their turn' (X, 791). Such ultra-republicanism, recalling John Lilburne's levellers in the English republican army of 1647, is also echoed by the 'thundering hoofs' across the Leven's 'level sand'.

(5)

In the course of 1974 Wordsworth believed that he had identified a school of English revolutionary thought that, though it was radically opposed to Pitt's national policies, could serve to reconcile the social idealism he had assimilated in France with a viable political programme at home: Godwinian philanthropism. Gradually, however, he came to see that its rationalistic basis had disturbing affinities with the abstract virtues of the revolution in whose name the Jacobins had ridden roughshod over deeply embedded social ties. In 1795–6 he suffered a moral and possibly nervous break-down as he came to the conclusion that all the political analyses with which he had become involved would lead to a society detached from the moral scheme of domestic and communal affections which he believed was bred from a close relation to nature, and demonstrated particularly by village life in the Lakes.

The story of the wonderful recovery of Wordsworth's own relation to nature, largely through seeing it mirrored in his sister Dorothy's intense susceptibility to her physical environment ('She gave me eyes, she gave me ears' ('The Sparrow's Nest' (1807), l.17; *PW*, I, 227) – first at Racedown, Dorset, then at Alfoxden, Somerset, and then, inevitably, back in the Lakes, at Dove Cottage, Grasmere, from 1800 – is for most readers the highpoint in the poet's life and writing. Wordsworth had returned to his past. In 1800, Coleridge wrote to a friend: 'I would to God, I could get Wordsworth to re-take Alfoxden – the Society of so Great a Being is a priceless Value – but he will never quit the North of England'.[18] And, of course, he never did. Rather, Coleridge moved north to Keswick, where the Southey family were already living. Together with a network of congenial neighbours and visitors, including especially the Hutchinson sisters, Mary and Sara, they made up a micro-community of high-mindedness, shared affection and nature-worship.

An important addition to this society was Wordsworth's favourite, mariner brother, Captain John Wordsworth, on visits between voyages. In many ways, he stood at the heart of its tender attachments: formerly in love with Wordsworth's future wife, Mary Hutchinson, and unofficially betrothed to her sister, Sara, with whom the married Coleridge was hopelessly in love. Two years younger than Wordsworth, John had also been at Hawkshead Grammar School, and Wordsworth saw in him another reminder of his former self, 'A silent poet' with a 'watchful heart . . . inevitable ear/And an eye practised like a blind man's touch' ('When to the attractions of the busy world', (finished 1802), ll.80–2; *PW*, II, 122), who took the sights and scenes of his Lakes childhood with him in memory on his voyages to China.

The plan for him to make the family's fortune and return to settle in the Grasmere community as Sara's husband was unrealised. In February 1805, *The Earl of Aber-gavenny*, the East Indiaman of which he was in charge, struck on the Shambles off Portland Bill, and, after a terrible storm which drove her on and off the reef, she sank. John Wordsworth, faithful to his duty, was swept overboard a few minutes before the end and drowned. It was the greatest shock to his regained equanimity that Wordsworth ever sustained. On one level this rupture of the family symbiosis that had been re-established in the landscape of their shared past marked the end of his retreat simply to rediscover his own lost peace of mind. To a friend he wrote: 'I feel that there is something cut out of my life which cannot be restored'.[19] As Stephen Gill has observed, Wordsworth returned repeatedly to the word 'fortitude' both to express John's spirit of active endeavour and his own responding sense of resolution.[20]

This development found exact expression the following year, 1806, when Wordsworth saw a painting, 'Storm: Peele Castle', in the London home of his patron, Sir George Beaumont, whose work it was. (Figure 1.5) The scene, of a ship threatened by a wrecking storm, represented, as Wordsworth immediately saw, the necessary revision of the picturesque idyll remembered from the summer of 1794. His poem, 'Elegiac Stanzas suggested by a Picture of Peele Castle, in a Storm, painted by Sir George Beaumont' (composed 1806) registers the contrast:

> Ah! THEN, if mine had been the Painter's hand,
> To express what then I saw; and add the gleam,
> The light that never was, on sea or land,
> The consecration, and the Poet's dream;
>
> I would have planted thee, thou hoary Pile
> Amid a world how different from this!
> Beside a sea that could not cease to smile;
> On tranquil land, beneath a sky of bliss.
>   . . .
> Not for a moment could I now behold
> A smiling sea, and be what I have been. (11.13–20, 37–8; *PW*, IV, 259–60)

But despite the rift between his idealising past and his present knowledge, Wordsworth

Figure 1.5: Sir George Beaumont, *Peele Castle*, 1806.
Private collection; reproduced with the owner's permission.

16

still needed to recover a sense of the scene as a locus of continuity, though one founded on new terms. The underlying structure of a nature-based morality was too deeply rooted to be disturbed, only the human frame of mind that was called upon to live up to it needed to be adjusted:

> O 'tis a passionate Work! – yet wise and well,
> Well chosen is the spirit that is here;
> That Hulk which labours in the deadly swell,
> This rueful sky, this pageantry of fear! (45–8)

Rather than diminishing the significance of human values, he argues, natural violence can bring them out:

> And this huge Castle, standing here sublime,
> I love to see the look with which it braves,
> Cased in the unfeeling armour of old time,
> The lightning, the fierce wind, and trampling waves.
>
> $\cdots$
>
> But welcome fortitude, and patient cheer,
> And frequent sights of what is to be borne!
> Such sights, or worse, as are before me here –
> Not without hope we suffer and we mourn. (49–52, 57–60)

It is, of course, the castle itself, as an image of survival, rather than the menaced ship, that opens up Wordsworth's alternative reading. He invents a history for it that transforms the scene into a reflection of a tradition of feeling that rather than being destroyed by nature, is empowered by it.

The martial bravery he attributes to it resonates with the contemporary national spirit of Trafalgar: Wordsworth claimed that his poem, 'Character of the Happy Warrior' (composed 1805 or 1806), was a composite portrait of his brother and Nelson.[21] But despite the island's strategically offering the best anchorage between Liverpool and the Solway, the castle had no recorded military history, being ungarrisoned during the times of the Armada, the Civil Wars, and the Napoleonic Wars. An original manor house had been given to Furness Abbey by King Stephen, and the abbot later obtained a license to crenellate, presumably to provide a place of refuge and a storehouse for church valuables. After several stages of decay and repair, however, it had fallen into ruin by the time of the dissolution of the monasteries, and the East Wall, which was gradually crumbling from the eighteenth to the nineteenth centuries, had completely gone by 1818. Its uses had been unheroic: in 1797, a commercial bakehouse had been constructed in the outer bailey, and the ravages it displayed were purely elemental.[22] Yet for Wordsworth, what the remnant had come to stand for was an unchanging human tradition ('Farewell, farewell the heart that lives alone,/Housed in a dream, at distance from the Kind!' (53–4) that matches up to, and proclaims its equivalence to the permanence of natural order – a deeply conservative longing that had perhaps been implicit in his increasingly idiosyncratic version of republicanism since the mid 1790s.

It was specifically towards Burke's great vision of a national tradition that Wordsworth's piety to his dead brother produced a strong individual urge. In his *Reflections on the Revolution in France* (1790), Burke had argued for the idea of inheritance, by which 'we have given to our frame of polity the image of a relation in blood; binding up the constitution of our country with our dearest domestic ties; adopting our fundamental laws into the bosom of our family affections'.[23] Wordsworth wrote of John: 'I shall never forget him, never lose sight of him, there is a bond between us yet, the same as if he were living, nay far more sacred, calling upon me to do my utmost, as he to the last did his utmost to live in honour and worthiness.'[24] Burke had described human society as 'a partnership' which 'cannot be obtained in many generations, it becomes a partnership not only between those who are living, but between those who are living, those who are dead, and those who are to be born',[25] and it was participation in this nation that in *The Prelude* Wordsworth promised Coleridge: 'There is/One great society alone on earth:/The noble living and the noble dead.' (X, 967–9)

As Gill has written, the 'trust, made sacred by his brother's death'[26] was the completion (never, however, achieved) of the great philosophical poem that was to make Wordsworth the great post-revolutionary teacher of the nation. On the North Lancashire coast he negotiated his new allegiance to the influence of the arch critic of the French Revolution – Edmund Burke. The region that had once mediated between his experience of the Lakes and the revolutionary society beyond had come to stand for the transformation of that natural culture into an opposite political tradition.

(6)

Burke was the propounder of an organic national tradition:

> Our political system is placed in just correspondence and symmetry with the order of the world, and with the mode of existence decreed to a permanent body composed of transitory parts; wherein, by the disposition of a stupendous wisdom, moulding together the great mysterious incorporation of the human race, the whole, at one time, is never old, or middle-aged, or young, but in a condition of unchangeable constancy, moves on through the tenour of perpetual decay, fall, renovation, and progression.[27]

The Burkean idea that, as Wordsworth put it, 'local attachment . . . is the tap-root of the tree of Patriotism'[28] tended to attribute nationalism to the same source to which Wordsworth attributed poetry: 'the spontaneous overflow of powerful feelings' (*PW*, II, 400). '(T)he poet', writes Wordsworth, 'binds together by passion and knowledge the vast empire of human society' (*PW*, II, 396). Such a capacity to articulate what came naturally was implied in what became the innocent empiricism of J. A. Seeley's famous aphorism that the British 'seem, as it were, to have conquered and peopled half the world in a fit of absence of mind.'[29] But Wordsworth had a doctrine of organicism which became defined as a critique of industrial capitalism – the other revolution, *within* the country, which was being produced by an economic system totally divorced from a founding relation with nature, and at war with the rural communities that put family and social ties first.

In Book Eight of *The Excursion* (1814), he drew a moving and influential portrait of a child-labourer from the factories of South Lancashire:

```
                      this organic frame,
So joyful in its motions, is become
Dull, to the joy of her own motions dead;
And even the touch, so exquisitely poured
Through the whole body, with a languid will
Performs its functions; rarely competent
To impress a vivid feeling on the mind
Of what there is delightful in the breeze,
The gentle visitations of the sun,
Or lapse of liquid element – by hand,
Or foot, or lip, in summer's warmth – perceived. (11.322–32; PW, V, 276)
```

In his distrust of industrial progress, Wordsworth was not shrinking from addressing the opportunity for world-wide influence that fell to an unopposed Britain after Waterloo; but he wished that power to spread from its roots in the pastoral economy. The spirit of national enterprise he sponsored was that of the timber-feller in Book Seven of *The Excursion* whose labour enabled the vegetational powering of the local navy of fishermen and coastal traders built in tiny ports such as Greenodd – Barrow was then a small hamlet – and an oddly organic version of the industrial machine:

```
                      Many a ship
Launched into Morecambe-bay, to *him* hath owed
Her strong knee-timbers, and the mast that bears
The loftiest of her pendants; He, from park
Or forest, fetched the enormous axle-tree
That whirls (how slow itself!) ten thousand spindles;
And the vast engine labouring in the mine,
Content with meaner prowess, must have lacked
The trunk and body of its marvellous strength,
If his undaunted enterprise had failed
Among the mountain coves. (11.602–12; PW, V, 250–1)
```

In this way, Wordsworth envisaged the ramification of empire, radiating out from the local culture of the Lakes. The Wanderer's vision of a universal 'humanised society' (1.389; PW, V, 298) in Book Nine of *The Excursion* is of this moral export:

```
'So wide the waters, open to the power,
The will, the instincts, and appointed needs
Of Britain, do invite her to cast off
Her swarms, and in succession send them forth;

                  . . .
– Vast circumference of hope – and ye
Are at its centre, British lawgivers'. (IX, 375–8, 398–9)
```

For Wordsworth, the crucial link between locality and national institutions was the church. A passage at the end of the second section of Wordsworth's *Guide* (first published in 1810), on the 'General Picture of Society' in the Lakes, reveals an interesting slippage between the kind of mountain republicanism from which Wordsworth had seen himself

Figure 1.6: Joseph Farington, *South View of Lancaster*, from his *The Lakes of Lancashire, Westmorland, and Cumberland*, 1816.

as descending and the extension of the boundaries of this rural commonwealth into the outer world of empire through a feudal establishment:

> Towards the head of these Dales was found a perfect Republic of Shepherds and Agriculturalists . . . The chapel was the only edifice that presided over these dwellings, the supreme head of this pure Commonwealth; the members of which existed in the midst of a powerful empire like an ideal society or an organized community, whose constitution had been imposed and regulated by the mountains which protected it. Neither high-born nobleman, knight, nor esquire was here; but many of these humble sons of the hills had a consciousness that the land, which they walked over and tilled, had for more than five hundred years been possessed by men of their name and blood; and venerable was the transition, when a curious traveller, descending from the heart of the mountains, had come to some ancient manorial residence in the more open part of the Vales, which, through the rights attached to its proprietor, connected the almost visionary mountain republic he had been contemplating with the substantial frame of society as existing in the laws and constitution of a mighty empire. (Pp.67–8)

Wordsworth's organic nationalism institutionalised nature. But in representing the institutions of the imperial state as 'natural', instead of effectively informing those institutions with a communitarian structure of feeling, he helped to create a version of British civilisation that, though it was increasingly ineffectual, (and *was* indeed marginalised), yet served to screen the political rationale of nationalism – the seeking of monopolies and the deflection abroad of social and economic conflicts – that Wordsworth actually opposed!

(7)

On the southern margin of De Quincey's 'fairy little domain', transitional between it and the other world of South Lancashire and beyond, lies Lancaster. Dominating the view, but at a distance unimposingly, stands Lancaster Castle. (Figure 1.6) In his *Guide*, Wordsworth noted that the point where it was possible to obtain

> a view of the fells and mountains of Lancashire and Westmorland; with Lancaster Castle, and the Tower of the Church seeming to make part of the Castle, in the foreground (p.3)

was the first sight of interest in the journey north of Preston. The castle is an ancient palimpsest of foundations and re-foundations from its Roman origin around 79 A.D., and the massy superstructure of the square keep which partly remains was built shortly after the Norman Conquest. From the first, it was an outpost of empire, a bastion of power driving northward against the Scots and Irish. Its most striking feature, the Gateway Tower, was built by the future King John, and subsequently enlarged and strengthened by John of Gaunt, second Duke of Lancaster, a statue of whom was inserted over the main entrance in 1822, and whose famous dying speech in *Richard II* sees the whole country as 'This fortress built by Nature for herself/Against infection and the hand of war' (II.i.43–4). (Figure 1.7) At least as early as the reign of Henry VIII it had become a prison, and by Wordsworth's day it had been the site of fifteen Roman Catholic martyrdoms; the place from which in 1612 the so-called witches were dragged to be hanged; the target of devastating batteries from Cromwell's armies; and a notorious debtors' prison.

Many famous trials were held there, such as that at the March Assizes of 1843, when Feargus O'Connor and 58 other Chartists were arraigned for encouraging strikes and 'creating alarm, discontent and confusion' at Manchester.[30] Thirty of those charged were sentenced to various terms of imprisonment, though, as was made explicit in some of the speeches in the eight-day trial, their demand for reform arose from their families' experience of factory conditions which were the social reality behind Wordsworth's own description in The *Excursion*.

Wordsworth's chief association with the castle, however, was that which attached to it for most people; as a centre for capital execution. Between 1799 and 1887, there were 228 hangings there. The sequence of poems which Wordsworth composed as his contribution to a topical debate on capital punishment in 1839–40, 'Sonnets Upon the Punishment of Death' (1841), opens with a poem entitled 'Suggested by the View of Lancaster Castle (on the Road from the South)'. It starts with the familiar response to the picturesque:

> *This Spot* – at once unfolding sight so fair
> Of sea and land, with yon grey towers that still
> Rise up as if to lord it over air –
> Might soothe in human breasts the sense of ill,

Figure 1.7: J. M. W. Turner, *The Gateway at Lancaster Castle*, from his *Views in Lancashire and Yorkshire, from original drawings*, 1872.

> Or charm it out of memory; yes, might fill
> The heart with joy and gratitude to God
> For all his bounties upon man bestowed.

But then he looks again at what lies behind the apparent loveliness:

> Why bears it then the name of 'Weeping Hill'?
> Thousands, as toward yon old Lancastrian Towers,
> A prison's crown, along this way they pass'd
> For lingering durance or quick death with shame,
> From this bare eminence theron have cast
> Their first look – blinded as tears fell in showers
> Shed on their chains; and hence that doleful name. (*PW*, IV, 135)

In 1823, around 100 felonies of the 200 that had been on the statute book were exempted from capital punishment, and in 1837 the Whig government removed the death penalty from all but four crimes, principally treason and murder. When the argument was made that murder also should be exempted, Wordsworth, showing what Mary Moorman describes as 'the same spirit of nervous dread of change which for many years now had overshadowed all his political views',[31] produced his meditative advocacy for its retention.

Wordsworth's overall approach to what the castle, as a seat of judicial power, should represent never loses sight of the original sense of blessed order over which the 'grey towers' preside. But in his manuscript '[An Unpublished Tour]' of the Lakes (1811–12?), the castle is described so as to shift from being seen *within* a picturesque setting to become the centre from which the whole panorama derives its sense of prestige:

> Lancaster with its Castle and its distant Mountains beyond present a grand picture to a Person approaching from the South, but noble as this landscape is, it is far inferior in its effect upon the mind to the panorama view from the principal Tower of the Castle itself. From this lofty station . . . the Spectator looks upon the inferior towers, courts, roofs, walls, battlements, & whole circumference of this vast edifice, & upon the town, shipping, aqueduct, & Bridge – works of art sufficiently splendid for the situation which they occupy in the centre of a magnificent prospect of sea and land.
> (*Prose*, II, 289–90,11.98–108)

As the castle exercises its surveillance over a picturesque panorama of the Irish Sea and the mountains of the Lakes, so, he urges in his sonnets, it should enact

Figure 1.8: 'Hanging' chair, Lancaster Castle. Made to support a young woman's walk to the gallows.

Reproduced with the permission of the *Westmorland Gazette*.

a 'moral code' that proceeds from the harmonious scheme of beauty and fear, ('As all Authority on earth depends/On Love and Fear' (*PW*, IV, 137), that the region had imparted to him from childhood. The moral beauty with which he invests institutional power is one imbued with the structure of his unchanging relation to nature.

The fourteen sonnets that make up this group sketch the generalised story of a crime and the best way that, all things considered, it should be dealt with: the victim's family's demand for redress, the 'absolute rule' of 'Honour' over 'the weak love of life' (*PW*, IV, 136), the beneficial workings of fear on the killer's conscience, the need to prevent private vendettas, the deteriorating effects of life imprisonment and the possibility of recidivism after banishment, the condemned man's acceptance of death as the road to salvation, and, finally, the likelihood of the crime dying out under the influence of Christianity. The narrative compresses into that of a willing victim, subjected to the benign discipline of the natural order: 'the wise Legislator's . . . Spirit, when most severe, is oft most kind' (*PW*, IV, 137). (Figure 1.8)

Wordsworth argues that the power of the state to 'fortify the moral sense of all' would be produced by extending the 'mental vision' from the site of capital punishment (*PW*, IV, 139)..In one manuscript of 'An Unpublished Tour', Wordsworth writes of the castle's 'majestic display of the coercive Power which cruel Society is compelled to exercise from this as a central point' (*Prose*, II, 290, n.127–33). But the reverence for moral severity that he sees as the upshot of the primary culture of the Lake District by the time he composed these sonnets had passed through a series of transformations, by which the state had come to appropriate, and cover up, its own institutional violence. On the border between region and nation, Wordsworth's 'nature' had been repeatedly translated into discourses of power, and had thereby moved gradually to the centre of the state. What in boyhood had been immediately repressed by the sacred at Furness Abbey had later returned as the expression of justified republican vengeance on the Leven estuary, and afterwards as the striving for a Burkean tradition of fortitude at Piel Castle. At Lancaster Castle, it becomes the disciplinary control behind state-power.

Wordsworth's treatment of this issue convincingly illustrates Michel Foucault's characterisation of the shift in the nineteenth-century state's technique of power, from punishment to discipline,[32] so that his story of an execution is one completely purified of gruesome spectacle and pain, shorn of the indignities and barbarities that contemporary eye-witness accounts record of a hanging crowd. It tends to the concealment of power rather than its excessive demonstration – power inscribed in the mind rather than on the body of the convict. Through the institutionalisation of nature, Wordsworth's Lakes had internalised this legal discipline (imitating the monastic and military disciplines of, for example, Furness and Piel), with the result that their tranquillising culture had effectively become a penitentiary.

Notes

1. The first use of the phrase 'Lake school' occurs in an article of August 1817 entitled 'Coleridge's *Literary Life*', *Edinburgh Review*, XXVIII. The name occurs in a note contributed by Francis Jeffrey as well as in the main text which was written by Hazlitt. The latter took up the 'denomination', 'the Lake school of poetry', in his lecture 'On the Living Poets' (1818).

   I am grateful to Dr. Robert Morrison for the following information: 'In the *General Index to the Edinburgh Review* (1813), the phrase '*Lake Poets*' appears as a heading. Two articles are listed under this heading, one of 1809 on Burns and one of 1812 on Wilson, both of which talk about the 'new school' (as had an 1802 review of Southey which also uses the term 'new sect') but neither of which contains the phrase 'Lake Poets'. That phrase at this point, it seems, is reserved solely for the index.' A review of Wordsworth, however, in the *Edinburgh Review* of October 1807, refers to 'a brotherhood of poets, who have haunted for some years about the Lakes in Cumerland', and a review by John Taylor Coleridge in the *Quarterly Review* of April 1814 uses the phrase 'the Lake Poets' several times. The term was to become established by De Quincey's *Recollections of the Lake Poets* (1854), a revised collection of articles that had been serialised in *Tait's Magazine* (1834–40), though the title was probably not his own. During 1839, De Quincey had entitled five articles in *Tait's* 'Lake Reminiscences, from 1807 to 1830'.

   Jeffrey, in his review of *The Excursion*, in the *Edinburgh Review* of November 1814, and Byron, in his dedication to *Don Juan* (1818), refer to the school as the 'lakers' (possibly in allusion to James Plumptre's comedy of that name (1798)).

Plumptre, however, used that term, as (De Quincey noted in a pocket-book) did 'the country people of that district', for '(t)hose who visit the Lakes, *not* those who reside amongst them'. See Peter A. Cook, 'Chronology of the "Lake School" Argument: Some Revisions', *RES* 28 (1977), 175–81.

2. Unless otherwise stated, all references to *The Prelude* are to the 1805 version in the Norton Critical Edition, edited by Jonathan Wordsworth, M. H. Abrams and Stephen Gill (New York and London, 1979).

3. *The Collected Writings of Thomas De Quincey*, 16 vols. (Edinburgh, 1862–71), I, 73–4. Further references to this edition thus: *Works.*

4. See Jonathan Wordsworth, *William Wordsworth, The Borders of Vision* (Oxford, 1982).

5. See Ronald Sands, Chapter 8, *Portrait of the Wordsworth Country* (London, 1984).

6. Note dictated to Isabella Fenwick, *The Poetical Works of William Wordsworth*, ed. Ernest de Selincourt, rev. Helen Darbishire, 5 vols. (Oxford, 1952–9), II, 522. Further references to this edition thus: *PW.*

7. Edited by Ernest de Selincourt (Oxford, 1977), p. 22. Further references to this edition: *Guide.*

8. Kenneth Smith, introduction to *Early Prints of the Lake District* (Nelson, 1973).

9. Peter Bicknell, *The Picturesque Scenery of the Lake District, Book Collector,* 36 (1987), p. 41. See also Jonathan Wordsworth, 'Thomas West', *Ancestral Voices: Fifty Books from the Romantic Period* (London and New York, 1991), pp. 16–17.

10. Quoted in Peter Bicknell, *Beauty, Horror and Immensity: Picturesque Landscape in Britain, 1750–1850* (Cambridge 1981), p. 1. This illustrated catalogue and Malcolm Andrews's *The Search for the Picturesque* (Aldershot, 1989) are the best introductions to the subject.

11. *Wordsworth's Hawkshead*, ed. Robert Woof (London, 1970). This should be supplemented by a small book by Eileen Jay, *Wordsworth at Colthouse: an account of the poet's boyhood years spent in the remote Lakeland hamlet of Colthouse* (Kendal, 1970). David McCracken gives a useful guide to the topography of the poems in *Wordsworth and the Lake District:*

A Guide to the Poems and their Places (Oxford, 1984).

12. See Mary Moorman, *William Wordsworth. A Biography: The Early Years 1770–1803* (Oxford, 1968), p. 68.

13. The 'circuit' referred to at line 136 is not that defined by the Norton editors, but that indicated by Gilpin:
'Round the whole runs an irregular wall, the boundary of the abbey, which crossing the valley in two places, and mounting its sides, makes a circuit of about two miles.' (*Observations* (London, 1793), I, 166–7).

14. Quoted by Alice Leach, *Furness Abbey: A History and Illustrated Guide* (Ulverston, 1988), p. 8.

15. Probably the road over Hay (or Watch) Hill, leading to the village of Isel, as suggested by many commentators including De Selincourt, Darbishire and the Norton editors. But see the counter-claims of Micklebrows in Eric Robertson, *Wordsworthshire: An Introduction to a Poet's Country* (London, 1911), pp. 32–3.

16. *The Spirit of the Age* (London, 1970), p. 132.

17. *The Poems of John Milton*, edited by John Carey and Alastair Fowler (London and Harlow, 1968), I, 485, 11.392–3.

18. To Thomas Poole, 21 March 1800, *The Collected Letters of Samuel Taylor Coleridge*, edited by E. L. Griggs, 6 vols. (Oxford, 1956–71), I, 582.

19. To James Losh, 16 March, 1805, *The Letters of William and Dorothy Wordsworth: the Early Years 1787–1805*, edited by Ernest de Selincourt, revised by Chester L. Shaver, p. 565. Further references thus: EY.

20. See *William Wordsworth: A Life* (Oxford, 1989), p. 240–1.

21. See the note dictated to Isabella Fenwick, *PW,* IV, 419.

22. See John F. Curwen, 'Piel Castle, Lancashire', and Rachel Newman, 'Excavations and Survey at Piel Castle, near Barrow-in-Furness, Cumbria', *Transactions of the Cumberland and Westmorland Antiquarian and Archaeological Society,* 10 (1910), pp. 271–87 and 87, pp. 101–116.

23. Edited by Conor Cruise O'Brien (Harmondsworth, 1968), p. 120.

24. To Sir George Beaumont, c.23 Feb. 1805, EY, p. 547.

25. *Reflections*, p. 120.

26. Gill, p. 241.
27. *Reflections,* p. 120.
28. *Essays upon Epitaphs,* III, *The Prose Works of William Wordsworth,* edited by W. J. B. Owen and J. W. Smyser, 3 vols. (Oxford, 1974), II, p. 93, 11.495–6. Further references thus: *Prose.*
29. *The Expansion of England,* ed. John Gross (Chicago and London, 1971), p. 12.
30. For facts about the castle, including a transcript of a speech by Pilling, one of the defendants, see Thos. Johnson in Collaboration with W. H Bingham, *All about Lancaster Castle: its annals and associations; and an account of all the more remarkable executions* (Blackburn, n.d.).
31. *William Wordsworth. A Biography: the Later Years 1803–1850* (Oxford, 1968), p. 535.
32. See *Discipline and Punish: the Birth of the Prison,* translated by Alan Sheridan (Harmondsworth, 1979).

Chapter Two

Coming Home: the Romantic Tradition of Mountaineering

David Craig

In his essay 'Climbers' the mountaineer Paul Nunn refers to 'the sensation familiar to many climbers after travelling in an alien country. As the mountain valleys open up and the distant snows glisten, on a winter night in Scotland or in early summer in the Soviet Caucasus, one feels that one is coming home.'[1] He is being unashamedly romantic, and rightly so, since our cult of the wilderness, untamed nature, the far-off and hard to reach, stems directly from the sensibility of the prime Romantic artists and thinkers, from Rousseau, Wordsworth, Coleridge, Beethoven, Turner. Before their time people were most likely to perceive steepness and remoteness as ugly, frightening or plain useless. When they did begin to relish them, they still held back in an exclamatory or gushing spectator role for two generations or so before they dared to go out onto the steeps and use their own limbs to grapple with them.

Mountains and crags had generally been thought of as the world at its least congenial to us humans. Even an early Swiss guidebook (1713) disparages the Alps because of their height, their perpetual snows, and their 'inconvenient and primitive' tracks[2] – precisely what we now flock there in our millions to enjoy. Two generations later, Samuel Johnson was ahead of his time in journeying deep into the Highlands and Islands of Scotland yet even he saw the visiting of 'rocks and heaths' as a philosophical duty (one must know everything) and not at all as a pleasure, since the 'untravelled wilderness' stood for nothing but 'the evils of dereliction', a 'wide extent of hopeless sterility', 'quickened only with one sullen power of useless vegetation':[3] the heather which now epitomises the allure of the Highlands for countless tourists. Richardson, the most perceptive novelist of the time, was at one with Johnson in equating rocky mountains with poverty, and Goldsmith (so eloquent in praise of a country way of life) greatly preferred the plains of the Netherlands to the Scottish Highlands where 'hills and rocks intercept every prospect'.[4]

Those very traditional attitudes aren't laughable, they are eminently reasonable. The steep places *are* uncomfortable, hard to live in, often barren or thin-soiled, sending down their spates of snow or boulders to crush the habitable ground below. In his *Voyage aux Pyrénées*, Taine, who was much closer to backward social conditions in western Europe than we are today, defined most lucidly the basis of the older revulsion from the highlands:

People who had just emerged from an era of civil war and semi-barbarism were reminded by them of hunger, of long journeys on horseback in rain and snow, of inferior black bread mixed with chaff, of filthy, vermin-ridden hostelries. They were tired of barbarism, as we are tired of civilisation . . .[5]

A generation after Taine, when a Swiss Alpine guide visited Leslie Stephen in London, the man of letters was taken aback when the working man found the view of roofs and smoking chimneys 'far finer' than the view of Mont Blanc. But as trains, tunnels, and steamboats delivered to the wild uplands more and more people with the leisure time to cultivate aesthetic pleasure as an end in itself, the habit of pleasuring ourselves amongst wildness at once took root and blossomed luxuriantly. Since then it has come to feel like a need.

Gray, the author of the 'Elegy Written in a Country Churchyard', travelled through the Lake District in 1768 and the journal that he published in 1775 is credited with helping to start the tourist boom. Thirty years before, he had had his first inkling of such an experience when he made the Grand Tour from France across the Alps into Italy and was staggered by the Grande Chartreuse: 'not a precipice, not a torrent, not a cliff, but is pregnant with religion and poetry.'[6] This prefigures Wordsworth and Coleridge, Keats and Byron. Yet Gray's key words still suggest the contradiction in his feelings for steeps.

Figure 2.1: Thomas Gainsborough, *Romantic Landscape with Sheep at a Spring*, 1783.
Reproduced with the permission of the Royal Academy of Arts.

He is charmed, he is repelled. The crags are 'savage', 'monstrous', 'horrible', and when he makes his famous tour through Borrowdale in 1768 he is almost comically ready to imagine dangers. Gowder Buttress at Lodore, the site of many rock routes including the excellent Fool's Paradise, is perceived as 'impending terribly', 'hanging loose and nodding forwards' and best passed by quickly and silently. True, it had let fall a chunk of rock onto the road several years before but the precautions he advises weren't going to have much actual effect on anything (except morale). What Gray is expressing is a vision of civilisation just managing to keep at bay the ogreish dangers that surround it, which both fascinate and alarm. A few years later that very urbane painter Gainsborough paints the same vision in his 'Romantic Landscape with Sheep at a Spring'(Figure 2.1): the two buttresses that overhang on the left are quite like Gowder in their vertical grain but we get little sense that the painter has seen these rocks. They're impressive props, suffused with pale-gold light to etherealise them and parted to show a green Eden beyond.

Writers were not yet able to make poetry directly out of the steep places: we can hardly count the florid rhetoric about the cliffs of Snowdonia in Gray's 'Bard'. This corresponds to the travellers' inability as yet to set their own feet and hands on the mountains. Gainsborough made his painting about a year before the first ascent of Mont Blanc in 1786. Most people still viewed the mountains from a distance, from their carriages, from boats on the lakes, through a Claude glass to compose the vista into a manageably pretty image. Fear of the wild uplands, albeit a 'delicious' one, still predominated because they weren't known at first hand. Even a naval veteran called Joseph Budworth, a sturdy walker who made the first recorded ascent of Harrison's Stickle in Great Langdale in 1797, 'insisted on bandaging his offside eye with his handkerchief'[7] before allowing himself to be led by a local lad across a steep slope.

According to Budworth's local informants, ' "they never remembered foine folk aiming at et afore" '[8] That is, the shepherds may well have climbed the mountains even to their summits and been as unimpressed by them, for all we know, as the Swiss guide was by Mont Blanc[9] The first person who fused the two approaches, workmanlike and aesthetic, local and touristic, was Wordsworth, a native-born Cumbrian who climbed rock as a boy in his foragings for birds' eggs. He evokes the experience in the first piece of climbing literature in English:

> In the high places, on the lonesome peaks,
> Where'er, among the mountains and the winds
> The mother-bird had built her lodge. Though mean
> My object and inglorious, yet the end
> Was not ignoble. Oh, when I have hung
> Above the raven's nest, by knots of grass
> And half-inch fissures in the slippery rock
> But ill sustained, and almost, as it seemed
> Suspended by the blast which blew amain,
> Shouldering the naked crag.[10]

Here the local lad was at home in the places which gave the tourists kittens even at a distance. It must simply have been natural for him to go there, as it was for Jim Birkett, doyen of Cumbrian rock-climbers, who also started climbing 'When I first started bird nesting – as soon as I was old enough to walk, practically'[11] and first learnt rope technique in order to get at the nests. Generations of boys before Wordsworth probably did the same; his way of turning it into poetry shows that the experience could now be claimed as valuable – fertile for your growth as a person. This was not on record before. In our time Jim Birkett, a down-to-earth man and not a poet, can say that 'if you love mountains you take an interest in everything they can give you,'[12] and we may say that the possibility of *loving* mountains dawned in the 1780s:

> at that time
> While on the perilous ridge I hung alone,
> With what strange utterance did the loud dry wind
> Blow through my ears; the sky seemed not a sky
> Of earth, and with what motion moved the clouds.(I, 346–50

In the famous passages that follow, about stealing a boat and skating on Ullswater, he evokes and then analyses the way in which experiences among the 'craggy Steeps' gave him his first crucial inklings of those irrational states, states of 'danger or desire' (I, 498), which come to stand for the gamut of what life is like, how it strikes us, how we take it. His guilty depression in the days after the mountain had seemed to stride after him as he rowed in the moonlight under a 'rocky steep'(I, 394), his elation as he seemed to see the rotation of the earth in the wheeling of the 'solitary cliffs'(I, 484) when he stopped skating in mid-glide: such were the moments that did most to form his image of the cosmos and himself in it.

Rousseau is often credited with first noticing, and acting upon, such perceptions and he too was brought up in mountain country. In 1728, journeying on foot to Italy from his birthplace in Geneva, he found in himself 'the strongest taste . . . for mountains especially'.[13] His *Confessions,* started in 1766, are far from dominated by wilderness experience but where he does touch on it the feeling is acutely modern. The plains can't count as beautiful: 'I need torrents, rocks, firs, dark woods, mountains, steep roads to climb or descend, abysses beside me to make me afraid.'[14] He knows the perversity of such experience and he revels in it: 'the amusing thing about my taste for precipitous places is that they make my head spin; and I am very fond of this giddy feeling so long as I am in safety.'[15] So he delights in what we now call boulder-trundling, or in spending hours on a bridge with a low parapet, looking hundreds of feet down at 'the foam and the blue water, whose roaring came to me amid the screams of ravens and birds of prey which flew from rock to rock'.[16] The conventional literary culture to which he still half-belonged was no help to him in making sense of all this: late in life he is still saying, 'at the sight of a beautiful mountain I feel moved, though I cannot say by what.'[17] However he is unmistakably at the source of Romanticism in his openness to experiences not classed as 'useful' by society and in his persistent belief that people could only become themselves if they shook off the more elaborate social conventions and lived, both working and relaxing, more amongst nature. In *Emile* he extols a life where people enjoy each other's hospitality 'in the garden . . . or on the banks of a running stream, in the fresh green grass'. Lewis Mumford, most humane of social thinkers, sees in this the germ of the picnic and the holiday – fundamental forms of urban relief and escape:

> The rambling, the botanizing, the geologizing . . . hours spent in feasting around the picnic hamper or sitting lazily around an almost primeval campfire . . . vacations in the Tyrol

climbing from Alpenhutte to Alpenhutte, or deep among the rocky walls of the Yosemite – all these delightful days were formulated by Rousseau and encouraged by his active example.[18]

From its origin this cult of the natural has had both a benign and a darker face. Amongst nature we can both reaffirm vitality – the energy which flows in the weather, plants, us animals – and also admit to the allure of whatever threatens us:

the more cultivated minds of the West began to incite fear and mystery within themselves . . . by pitting themselves against the elements: going abroad in thunderstorms, with the lightning streaking across their path, climbing high mountains even above the snowline, exploring caves: in short, doing for an esthetic reason the same undaunted actions that the sailor, the peasant, the woodsman, or the miner were wont to do in the course of their works and days.[19]

Rousseau, again ahead of his time, had hinted at this when he said to Boswell in 1764, 'There's the great matter, to have force.'[20] Such a concept almost excludes ethics: any flow of impulse is exalted, regardless of consequences. Sheer intensity of living becomes the supreme goal. Here is the credo of those Extreme climbers in America who are so much readier than their British counterparts to articulate their views as a drastic philosophy: for example Mark Wilford when he says in the *Cloudwalker* film,

If you knew that however stupid your actions were you weren't going to die, the experience would be much less, like riding a roller-coaster in Disneyland . . . I don't want to stop climbing – I want it to end in the mountains . . . I like to operate near the edge of what I can do, so someday, unless I'm incredibly lucky, or just quit, I'm going to fall over that fine line.[21]

This pursuit of intensity through risk is already unmistakable in the first piece of climbing prose in English: a letter Coleridge wrote to Sarah Hutchinson on August 6 1802, the day after making the first recorded ascent of Sca Fell. He begins the letter by admitting that he courts danger, a 'sort of Gambling . . . not of the least criminal kind for a man who has children'. When he has to climb down a mountain, he doesn't look for a path but 'wanders on relying upon fortune'.[22] It was this habit, pure Romanticism in its spontaneity, that led him down the rockclimb called Broad Stand, a series of ten and fifteen-foot steps and smooth rectangular corners which rise up from the col between Sca Fell and Scafell Pikes. It is now graded Moderate and I've seen notices in Lake District shops warning walkers not to climb it without a rope.

Coleridge's prose, like the latest American climbing writing, plunges us into the midstream of his experience, a headlong physical spate in which instant follows instant so quickly that the Latinate syntax of the time breaks into a staccato of simple clauses:

I began to suspect that I ought not to go on, but then unfortunately tho' I could with ease drop down a smooth Rock 7 feet high, I could not *climb* it, so go on I must, and on I went, the next 3 drops were not half a Foot, at least not a foot more than my own height, but every Drop increased the Palsy of my Limbs – I shook all over, Heaven knows without the least influence of Fear – and now I had only two more to drop down, to return was impossible – but of these two the first was tremendous, it was twice my own height, & the Ledge at the bottom was so exceedingly narrow, that if I dropt down upon it I must of necessity have fallen backwards & of course killed myself.[23]

By now he was trembling too much to go on. As he writes we see how this negative state mutates into a positive one: the raised adrenalin flow fuels a high and a Romantic epiphany or visionary moment is born of it:

I lay upon my Back to rest myself, & was beginning according to my Custom to laugh at myself for a Madman, when the sight of the Crags above me on each side, & the impetuous Clouds just over them, posting so luridly & raptly northward, overawed me, I lay in a state of almost prophetic Trance & Delight – & blessed God aloud for the powers of Reason & the Will, which remaining no Danger can overpower us! O God, I exclaimed aloud – how calm, how blessed am I now, I know not how to proceed, how to return, but I am calm & fearless & confident, if this Reality were a Dream, if I were asleep, what agonies had I suffered! What screams! – When the Reason & the Will are away, what remain to us but Darkness & Dimness & a bewildering Shame, and Pain that is utterly Lord over us, or fantastic Pleasure, that draws the Soul along swimming through the air in many Shapes, even as a Flight of Starlings in a Wind.[24]

Reinvigorated, he climbed on down to the col of Mickledore, past a rotting sheep and through the final chimney, which is so narrow that he had to slide his knapsack to one side to avoid getting stuck.

It's typical of Coleridge's intelligence that even while he seems to be letting emotions run riot, he can be clear with himself that the experience demanded reason – a 'calm confidence' – if it was not to get out of hand and ruin him. The point is absolutely relevant to climbing, in which physical surge and exact appraisal of the terrain have to mesh. He is also very much the Romantic in his courting of extreme experiences, as Shelley was twenty years later when he went out into the Gulf of Leghorn in a small sailing-boat as a storm blew up and was drowned, or Turner in 1842, in his rather more craftsmanly way, when he got the material for his tremendous vortical 'Snowstorm' painting by asking 'the sailors to lash me to the mast to observe it; I was lashed for four hours, and I did not expect to escape, but I felt bound to record it, if I did.'[25] As Coleridge lost height beneath the 'enormous & more than perpendicular Precipices and *Bull's-Brows* of Sca'Fell' – a perfect description of the barrel-shaped East Buttress – a thunderstorm began to break and triggered off another epiphany:

Such Echoes! O God! what thoughts were mine! O how I wished for Health & Strength that I might wander about for a Month together in the stormiest month of the year, among these Places, so lonely & savage & full of sounds!

And he shouted out the names of his family, exulting in the extraordinary 'distinctness & *humanness* of Voice' which the mountain walls gave back.[26] He is embracing chaos, making himself at home in it.

A month later he makes the first analysis of climbing psychology. On a day of gusting wind and rain squalls he climbed at Newlands Hause, probably with Charles and Mary Lamb, keeping so close to the edge of Moss Force that he jagged his hands on the rock. He welcomed the fierce conditions because 'I have always found this *stretched & anxious* state of mind favorable to depth of pleasurable Impression, in the resting places & *lounding* Coves'[27], i.e. on the stances where the foregoing tensions can turn into something to be savoured. So the 'Impression', or enjoyed sensation, has become an end in itself, a state to be gone out after and got.

The aesthetics of this are pure Rousseau: like him, Coleridge puts himself in the way of dizzy feelings and delights in the force of waterfalls. On Moss Force he writes,

> What a sight it is to look down on such a Cataract! – the wheels, that circumvolve in it – the leaping & plunging forward of that Infinity of Pearls & Glass Bulbs – the continual *change* of the *Matter,* perpetual *Sameness* of the *Form*.[28]

He is at an age of development beyond Rousseau in his ability to 'say what he is moved by'. Yet he is still some way short of Wordsworth. The scholar A. P. Rossiter – who put up the Wasdale climb called The Gargoyle – has shown that Coleridge melted down his Newlands experience into the poem he published a month later, called 'Hymn Before Sunrise, in the Vale of Chamouni'. He pretended that he had 'involuntarily poured forth' the 'Hymn' while he was on Sca Fell but afterwards thought 'the Ideas &c disproportionate to our humble mountains' and transplanted them 'to these grander external objects'[29] – Mont Blanc, the River Arve, the glaciers. The result in the rendering of heightened experience is pure loss. The stock bombast of the waterfall imagery in 'Hymn' – 'Unceasing thunder and eternal foam'[30] and so on – can't compare with the original in his letter: 'in twilight one might have feelingly compared them to a vast crowd of huge white Bears, rushing, one over the other, against the wind – their long white hair shattering abroad'.[31] And when he interprets the experience all he can offer is a kind of hysterical piety, full of 'Awake, my soul!' and 'Thou too, hoar Mount!'[32] The quality of the thinking is infant-school hymn, orchestrated for invisible choir. God is credited with making the flowers and the rainbows, one thing after another is exhorted to utter 'GOD!', and torrents and eagles, ice-falls and lightning, are enlisted in the general roll-call until 'Earth, with her thousand voices, praises GOD.'[33] The result is neither vivid nature poetry nor convincing philosophy.

In contrast Wordsworth evokes the Alpine countryside in rich detail when he writes in 1805 about crossing the Simplon Pass many years before:

> The immeasurable height
> Of woods decaying, never to be decayed,
> The stationary blasts of waterfalls
> And everywhere along the hollow rent
> Winds thwarting winds, bewildered and forlorn
> The torrents shooting from the clear blue sky,
> The rocks that muttered close upon our ears,
> Black drizzling crags that spake by the wayside
> As if a voice were in them.(VI, 556–64)

Description then builds to a philosophical climax; where Coleridge was merely inspirational, Wordsworth is cogent, working with clear and valid concepts:

> Tumult and peace, the darkness and the light,
> Were all like workings of one mind, the features
> Of the same face, blossoms upon one tree,
> Characters of the great apocalypse,

The types and symbols of eternity,
Of first, and last, and midst, and without end. (567–72).

At such points Wordsworth is taking poetry over a watershed into a new mental country. He is having a crucial experience amongst raw nature – a place which has not been brought into the scope of human meanings by cultivation or buildings or even prior myth. There is nothing social to underwrite its significance. He doesn't idealise it as Arcadia in the manner of the Classical poets or absorb it into civilisation as his Augustan forerunners had done by concocting a language based on artifice ('floating Forests paint the Waves with Green'[34] and so on). All that guarantees the value of Wordsworth's experience is his ability to find striking words for heartfelt states of mind, and these could occur (as he emphasises himself) at the most ordinary spots among the Cumbrian mountains – beside a pool on a bare common near Penrith, for example, or in the shelter of a stone wall near Hawkshead in the company of a sheep and a blasted hawthorn (XI, 301–15, 349–63).

In terms of origins the difference between the two poets is that Wordsworth climbed rock first as a boy and a youth and knew the uplands intimately over decades, whereas Coleridge climbed on just a few occasions, as a short-term resident near Keswick, almost as a tourist. There flows from them two different but kindred ways of perceiving and frequenting the steeps. Wordsworth understands them as 'local habitations' which have their own culture and entwine themselves over the years with a person's growth until they stand for his vision of life's phases and possibilities. Coleridge reacts to them as sites of heightened sensation, opportunities for ecstasy and dread and thrill. Coleridge's way can be seen as the forerunner of the climbing literature that stresses ego and the private high rather than the nature amongst which we do the experiencing. Wordsworth's way anticipates the literature that finds a source of truths and values in the organic world. The former kind includes the writers about Extreme rock who have drawn styles and attitudes from Modernism and the drug culture; the latter includes Menlove Edwards and W. H. Murray.

Between the Romantics and the moderns there lies, of course, a long trend of evolving attitudes and it is worth noticing some of the landmarks on the way. In 1825 a guidebook to the Lakes opined that Pillar Rock in Ennerdale was 'unclimbable'. By the end of the following year four local shepherds had reached its summit[35] – firstcomers in a tradition of rubbishing the 'unclimbable' guidebook label that flourishes to this day. In the 1840s two more Romantic poets, Matthew Arnold and A. H. Clough, went up Helvellyn and some members of their party tried a rock-climb on Eagle Crag, Grisedale, a steep outcrop where Jim Birkett put up the last of his routes in the summer of 1954. Between 1850 and 1875 climbs of Pillar rose from two a year to fifty. In 1857 the Alpine Club was founded. The Wetterhorn was climbed by Wills in 1854, the Matterhorn by Whymper in 1865. In America the value of wilderness, philosophised by Thoreau, was built into an institution with the founding of Yellowstone National Park in 1872. Lliwedd's west buttress was first climbed, by Stocker and Wall, in January 1883 and in June 1886 Haskett Smith climbed Napes Needle in Wasdale. These break-outs from the gullies onto the faces of the cliffs set in motion the practice of steep cragging which has never let up from that day to this. During that decade other wilderness activities started up – pot-holing, seacliff climbing, small-boat sailing – and between 1879 and 1893 Mummery climbed the Matterhorn by six different routes and the Grepon without a guide, on the strength of which he can be credited with creating modern mountaineering. In 1890 Yosemite became part of a National Park in California and five years later the National Trust was set up, with a Cumbrian vicar as its first secretary, to manage places of historic interest and natural beauty for the benefit of the nation. At the same time skiing was quite suddenly becoming popular in centres like Chamonix.

All this had been happening as Britain changed under the onset of the factory system. In 1790 twice as many people lived in the country as in the towns. By 1830 the opposite was the case.[36] And the cities, growing at breakneck speed, were desperately congested, creating a need for space and refreshment, as did the long, enforced hours in the mills. A Lancashire weaver, John Grimshaw, epitomised the condition of millions in two lines of a song:

> You musn't walk in your gardens for two or three hours a-day.
> For you must stand at their command, and keep your shuttles in play.[37]

By the middle of the century rural depopulation was felt to be serious in outlying counties such as Dorset and Cumberland. As people drained away from the dales and the highlands, they also began to flock back for short, idyllic spells: the holiday was invented. It's in this context of growing leisure time, enjoyed at first by the upper and middle classes, that the cult of wild uplands becomes potent, in some cases almost religious.

The best (the only?) living representative of the 'Wordsworthian' tradition is W. H. Murray, a workmanlike historian and novelist as well as a major pioneer of ice and rock routes in Scotland just before and after the Second World War. His twin climbing books, *Mountaineering in Scotland* (1947) and *Undiscovered Scotland* (1951), not only chronicle the old Spartan days when gentleman-climbers referred to each other by their surnames, chopped steps with long-handled ice-axes, swam in mountain lochans before embarking on new thousand-foot routes, and drank Mummery's Blood (a mixture of rum and boiling Bovril) when they got back to the tent in a blizzard; they also seek to interpret peaks of experience in the light of an exalted metaphysical philosophy. Murray's favourite mountain, Buachaille Etive Mor, seen brilliantly moonlit in midwinter, is 'less clogged with the pollutions of mortality than is normally granted to an earthly form'.[38] In the course of this essay, 'Evidence of Things Not Seen', the mountains all around come alive for him. He feels 'their rough honesty go straight to his heart' where it kindles 'a contentment of the same kind, if less high, as that where friendship of two men ripens until the delight of simple companionship removes the need of speech.'[39] When the cloud-sea parts, the lochans on Rannoch Moor become 'hosts of white eyes upturned, calmly looking to the moon'.[40]

Such anthropomorphism comes naturally to Murray, as to all Romantics. At one level it is a vein of metaphor, mined for images that will embody, by projection, the intensity of the writer's feelings among crags and peaks. So Menlove Edwards, in his essay 'End of a Climb' (1937), sees the cliffs and trees above Llanberis as animate beings:

> The arms of the sun, as if driven into quick motion, lifted their beams clear of the earth, and the particles of their warmth, despairing, concentrated their last effort in a soft rose light along the western aspect of the strip of cloud. Down on the rocks a squat yew tree, clinging to the face, shivered and drew itself up. The shadows came together and lay cramped stiffly over it.

We turned our backs finally to the hills and began to chatter: setting about to make our minds easy. But behind us, fighting their slow wars, the forces of nature also shifted steadily on.[41]

So Murray hears 'the whole creation', including the clouds and the hills, throbbing 'with a full and new life; its music one song of honour to the beautiful',[42] or again (after doing the first ascent of Parallel Buttress on Lochnagar), 'One heard it circle the world like a lapping tide, the wave-beat of the sea of beauty; and as we listened from our watch tower and looked out across the broad earth, our own little lives and our flush of triumph in climbing a new route became very trivial things.'[43] So far, so conventional. The 'wave-beat of the sea of beauty' is a marvellous Romantic phrase but the 'little lives' idea, entertained as usual at sunset, is a well-worn pebble from the stream of mountain writing, to be found in Leslie Stephen's 'Sunset on Mont Blanc',[44] in Edwards' 'End of a Climb' (finely expressed: 'We were small to that. So many generations has man been lifting the stones, little stones, big stones, to clear a small pasture'[45]), and in a hundred other places. At this point, however, Murray 'contradicts' himself and a strong thought comes of it:

> Yet in that same instant our climb on the granite crags, the bare summit and the lands below, were with ourselves idealized as though in a point out of time and exalted in oneness. We began to understand, a little less darkly, what it may mean to inherit the earth.[46]

This concept of 'oneness' is from the Romantic mainstream: Wordsworth's perception in *The Prelude* that all those features of the Alps south of the Simplon were 'like workings of one mind . . . blossoms upon one tree,' or Shelley's vision in 'Adonais':

> The One remains, the many change and pass;
> Heavens's light forever shines, Earth's shadows fly;
> Life, like a dome of many-coloured glass,
> Stains the white radiance of eternity.[47]

In 'Rocks and Realities' Murray draws on Keats's 'Ode on a Grecian Urn' to affirm that the deep aim of climbing is to 'win fleeting glimpses of that beauty which all men who have known it have been compelled to call truth.'[48] Beauty, truth and oneness, throughout his two books, figure as the same. In his essay on the first ascent of Leac Mhor, the Great Slab on Garbh Bheinn in Ardgour, he writes: ' "My One Beauty is in all things." By the light of the beacon read the word on the mountainface'.[49] In 'Effects of Mountaineering on Men' he says that beauty, in climbing literature, goes with 'a certainty of the universal unity' or a 'premonition of an ultimate reality, the spiritual ground of things seen.'[50]

Although my respect for Murray's understanding of the mountains (and for the whole of Scotland, especially the islands) could hardly be greater, I'd have to demur at such passages, and finally part company with them, because they lose sight of the earth itself. (Figure 2.2) In 'The Undiscovered Country' he records how, squatting in a slit trench in the Libyan desert of 1942, he had an epiphany of mountains:

> I could see a great peak among fast-moving cloud, and the icy glint where its snow caught the morning sun. There were deep corries and tall crags. All of these were charged with a beauty that did not belong *to them,* but poured through them as light pours through the

glass of a ruby and blue window, or as grace through a sacrament.[51]

Shelley again! *This world is* being dislimned, blurred, conjured nearly away, and lofty chimeras take its place. Now we see them, now we don't. On the Buachaille, after being flooded with that sublime mountainscape seen by moonlight over cloud, Argyll and Lochaber visible like 'iceberg islands' and the Rannoch Wall 'pale as shadowed milk, impregnably erect', Murray still hankered after his 'ultimate reality':

> I came down from the summit filled with the acute awareness of an imminent revelation lost; a shadow that stalked at my side ever more openly among the hills. Something underlying the world we saw had been withheld. The very skies had trembled with presentiment of that reality; and we had not been worthy.[52]

'No, no, *no*,' I want to say to him. 'You *had* been worthy of the mountain, by being up there at all. *No* world was withheld; all there was to see, you saw. The beauty *did* belong to them – it *was* them.' For isn't this the truth, which Murray, with his tremendous feeling for the steep places, should be better fitted to see than anybody: that reality is not 'ultimate' at all, it is wholly present? That Welsh rock which bulks out of the fog, its mass rooted deep in the shingle, its sea-worn faces still bearing the stress-marks of its prehistoric forging and tempering, is not a faulty copy of some ideal Rock with a capital R, which

Figure 2.2: David Craig and Bill Peascod on Dexter Wall, Grey Crag, Birkness, June 1982.
Photograph by Chris Culshaw.

37

lurks somehow, somewhere, on some other plane. There is no Rock, there are only all the particular rocks that stand up out of (or lie still undisclosed in) this tangible planet which is our habitat:

> the very world which is the world
> Of all of us, the place in which, in the end,
> We find our happiness, or not at all. (X, 725–7)

The 'imminent revelation' is never 'lost'. (Figure 2.3) It is there for us to see continuously, at all times, in this rock and in that: in *this* iron-dark scimitar-blade (the last pitch of Centaur on Sca Fell East Buttress) which I grip so strongly to layback up it that my finger-bones wince at its serrations; in *that* corner, indented in the mountain's brow (on Pinnacle Face, Lochnagar), a thick old piton made by some Buchan blacksmith planted in its joint, which secretes oil-black ooze as though hellbent on slithering us off; in *this* pitted rockface (Buckbarrow in Longsleddale) which looks as though shrapnel has been blasted at it to make toothed pockets for the toes; in *that* summit-pile of bone-white quartzite chunks (Spidean a Choire Leith on Liathach) which once, in 1977, so buzzed with static that Julie's hair flew outwards and each lock bristled at its tip like a lightning conductor; in *that* burnished yew bole (on the fourth stance of Overhanging Bastion, Castle Rock of Triermain) which has been so grasped and tied onto by happy, sweating hands that its bared roots splay above the rock-shelf like a stranded arthropod . . . That tree, that summit, that face, that corner, that edge – from those very ones, and their billion

Figure 2.3: David Craig and Bill Peascod on 'Haste Not', White Gill, Great Langdale, August 1983.
Photograph by Chris Culshaw.

siblings, the world is composed. We will find nothing else, however much we yearn and hanker, and we need nothing else. Those crystals and fibres, masses and edges, great graved bulks and exquisitely chiselled details are the parts of the only world there is and the whole of that world is their sum. Nothing of it is 'withheld' (or not forever) and nothing 'underlies' it, except its core, six thousand kilometres in, where rock is three million times as dense as on the surface, and Murray does not mean that!

Notes

1. Paul Nunn, 'Climbers': *Climber and Rambler (Glasgow, April 1980)*, p. 32.
2.. Leslie Stephen, *The Playground of Europe* (London, 1871), pp. 1–2.
3. Samuel Johnson, *A Journey to the Western Highlands of Scotland*, 1775, edited by J.D.Fleeman (Oxford, 1985), pp. 30–2.
4. Stephen, pp. 9–10.
5. Quoted by G.Plekhanov, *Unaddressed Letters + Art and Social Life* (Moscow, 1957), p. 30.
6. *The Works of Thomas Gray*, 2 vols. (London, 1825), II, 61.
7. Tom Bowker, *Mountain Lakeland* (London, 1984), pp. 203–4.
8. *Ibid.*
9. Stephen, p. 1.
10. *The Prelude,. 1799, 1805, 1850*, edited by Jonathan Wordsworth, M.H.Abrams, and Stephen Gill (New York, 1979), p. 46, ll.337–46.
11. Bill Birkett, 'Talking with Jim Birkett': *Climber and Rambler* (Glasgow, August 1982), p. 25.
12. *Ibid.*
13. *The Confessions of Jean-Jacques Rousseau*, 1781, translated by J.M.Cohen (London, 1953), p. 64.
14. *Ibid.*, p. 167.
15. *Ibid.*
16. *Ibid.*, pp. 167–8.
17. *Ibid.*, p. 593.
18. Lewis Mumford, *The Condition of Man*, 1944 (London, 1963), pp. 297–8.
19. *Ibid.*, p. 280.
20. *Boswell on the Grand Tour*, edited by F.A.Pottle (London, 1953), p. 218.
21. Quoted from soundtrack of *Cloudwalker*, directed by Michael Tobias (1982).
22. *Collected Letters of Samuel Taylor Coleridge*, 6 vols., edited by Earl Leslie Griggs (Oxford, 1956–71), II, 841.
23. *Ibid.*, p. 842.
24. *Ibid.*
25. Graham Reynolds, *Turner* (London, 1969), p. 190.
26. Coleridge, *Letters*, II, 843–4.
27. *Ibid.*, p. 853.
28. *Ibid.*
29. *Ibid.*, p. 854 n.1, p. 865.
30. Coleridge, *Selected Poetry and Prose*, edited by Stephen Potter (london, 1950), p. 110.
31. Coleridge, *Letters*, II, 853.
32. Coleridge, *Selected Poetry and Prose*, pp. 110–11.
33. *Ibid.*
34. Alexander Pope, 'Windsor Forest', l.210; *The Poems*, edited by John Butt (London, 1963), p. 202.
35. Alan Hankinson, *The First Tigers*, 1972 (Bassenthwaite, 1984), pp. 35–6.
36. G.D.H.Cole and Raymond Postgate, *The Common People*, 1946 (London, 1956), p. 305; Lewis Mumford, *The City in History* (London, 1966), p. 532.
37. 'Hand-loom v. Power-loom', *Ballads and Songs of Lancashire*, edited by John Harland (London, 1882), p. 189.
38. Murray, double volume (London, 1979), 1/p. 122.
39. *Ibid.*, 1/p. 244.
40. *Ibid.*, 1/p. 225–6.
41. Jim Perrin, *Menlove* (London, 1985), p. 351.
42. Murray, 1/pp. 226–7.
43. *Ibid.*, 1/p/129.
44. Stephen, pp. 227–8, 285.
45. Perrin, p. 316.
46. Murray, 1/p. 129.
47. *The Complete Poetical Works of Percy Bysshe Shelley*, edited by Thomas Hutchinson (Oxford, 1934), p. 443.
48. Murray, 1/p. 242.

49. *Ibid.*, 2/p. 65.
50. *Ibid.*, 2/p. 223.
51. *Ibid.*, 2/p. 7.
52. *Ibid.*, 2/p. 226.

Chapter Three

Charles Dickens, John Ruskin and the old King's Arms Royal Hotel, Lancaster, with Seven Letters to its Landlord Mr. Joseph Sly.

David Steel

In August 1857 a programme of exacting public readings of *A Christmas Carol* and Wilkie Collins's *The Frozen Deep*, given in Manchester, had reduced Dickens to a state of temporary mental exhaustion. On the 29th, restless and depressed, he wrote to Collins, his favourite companion of the time, humorously urging him to come away with him

> anywhere – take any tour – see anything – whereon we could write something together. Have you any idea tending to any place in the world? Will you rattle your head and see if there is any pebble in it which we could wander away and play at marbles with? We want something for *Household Words* and I want to escape from myself.[1]

Dickens needed the change and the rest. *Household Words*, the magazine he had founded seven years earlier, and to which Collins was a fellow contributor, needed material. In short relaxation and inspiration were sought together.

It was to Collins, whom he had first met in 1851, that Dickens was inclined to turn for distracting and energetic relief from the problems of his marriage which was later to break down completely. Dickens was now forty-five and a famous name. Collins, in 1857, was thirty-three and still at the outset of his literary career with his major novels *The Woman in White*, *No Name*, *Armadale*, and *The Moonstone* yet to come. A proposal to escape was not to be resisted and the pair promptly left for the Lakeland Fells on what the prime mover of the trip called 'a little tour in search of an article and in avoidance of railroads.[2]

But trains were not easy to avoid and the two travelled by rail as far as Carlisle, from there to Wigton and on to Allonby on the Cumbria coast overlooking the Solway Firth. With an Allonby innkeeper for guide, who proved to have as much knowledge of the lie of the land as they had, Dickens dragged the less enthusiastic Collins to the summit of Carrock Fell where they lost their way in the mist and where, as they scrambled along the bed of a stream in an attempt to find their way down, Collins sprained his ankle. The descent was slow and painful and the stalwart Dickens had to carry his injured companion a good part of the way. Back at the hotel limbs and morale were somewhat eased when both Collins's foot and Dickens's throat were plied with whisky. After two days' rest in their 'capital little homely inn', rest, that is, for Collins, while the irrepressible Dickens frenziedly explored the surrounding area, the pair returned to Carlisle on Friday 11th September with the intention of travelling on to Lancaster the following day.[3] It was from the County Hotel in Carlisle that Dickens wrote the following letter:

> Mr. Charles Dickens sends his compliments to the master of the King's Arms at
> Lancaster, and begs to say that he wishes to bespeak for *tomorrow* (*Saturday*)
> afternoon and night, a private sitting-room and two bedrooms; also a comfortable
> dinner for two persons at half past 5. Mr. Dickens will be accompanied by his friend
> Mr. Wilkie Collins; and as Mr. Collins has unfortunately sprained his leg, it will be a
> great convenience for him to have his bedroom as near the sitting-room as possible.
> For the same reason Mr. Dickens will be glad to find a fly awaiting them at the station.
> They purpose leaving here by the mid-day train at 12.38.
> County Hotel
> Friday evening
> Eleventh September 1857.[4]

Although Dickens was a connoisseur of fine old inns, many of which figure, transposed or not, in his fiction, the King's Arms Royal Hotel at Lancaster and its landlord were to prove rather special. Sitting in his room there after early dinner on the evening of Saturday 12th September and writing to 'Georgy', Georgina Hogarth (his sister-in-law), he noted:

> We are in a very remarkable old house here, with genuine old rooms and an uncommonly
> quaint staircase. I have a state bedroom, with two enormous red four-posters in it, each
> as big as Charley's room at Gad's Hill. Bellew is to preach here tomorrow. 'And we know
> he is a friend of yours Sir,' said the landlord, when he presided over the serving of the
> dinner (two little salmon trout; a sirloin steak; a brace of partridges; seven dishes of sweets;
> five dishes of dessert, led off by a bowl of peaches; and in the centre an enormous
> bride-cake – 'We always have it here, Sir', said the landlord, 'custom of the house'.)
> Collins turned pale, and estimated the dinner at half a guinea each'.[5]

His imagination fired by the curious old room in which he found himself, and perhaps transposing Collins's financial fears into terrors of a more supernatural sort, Dickens sat up all night to write the ghost story of *The Bride's Chamber* a section of *The Lazy Tour of Two Idle Apprentices*, the writing of which was one of the reasons for the journey to the North-West.

Produced in collaboration with Collins, and first published in *Household Words* in October 1857, *The Lazy Tour* gives a fictionalized account of the adventures of the two travellers under the names of Thomas Idle and Francis Goodchild. The stay at Allonby, the ramble up Carrock Fell, the mishap in the mist are all transposed in threadbare disguise. The two travellers having come to a short halt on their tour, Idle has no doubt as to where they should next direct their steps, managing in his proposal to include a jaundiced reference to the discomforts of marriage:

> 'I have heard there is good old Inn, at Lancaster, established in a fine old house: an Inn
> where they give you Bride-cake every day after dinner . . . Let us eat Bride-cake without
> the trouble of being married, or of knowing anybody in that ridiculous dilemma'.
>
> Mr. Goodchild, with a lover's sigh, assented. They departed from the station in a violent

hurry . . . and were delivered at the fine old house at Lancaster on the same night.

It is Mr. Goodchild's opinion, that if a visitor on his arrival at Lancaster could be accommodated with a pole which would push the opposite side of the street some yards further off, it would be better for all parties. Protesting against being required to live in a trench, and obliged to speculate all day upon what the people can possibly be doing within a mysterious opposite window, which is a shop window to look at, but not a shop window in respect of its offering nothing for sale and declining to give any account whatever of itself, Mr. Goodchild concedes Lancaster to be a pleasant place. A place dropped in the midst of a charming landscape, a place with a fine ancient fragment of castle, a place of lovely walks, a place possessing staid old houses richly fitted with old Honduras mahogany, which has grown so dark with time that it seems to have got something of a retrospective mirror-quality into itself, and to show the visitor, in the depths of its grain, through all its polish, the hue of the wretched slaves who groaned long ago under old Lancaster merchants. And Mr. Goodchild adds that the stones of Lancaster do sometimes whisper, even yet, of rich men passed away – upon whose great prosperity some of these old doorways frowned sullen in the brightest weather – that their slave-gain turned to curses, as the Arabian Wizard's money turned to leaves, and that no good ever came of it, even unto the third and fourth generations, until it was wasted and gone. It was a gallant sight to behold, the Sunday procession of the Lancaster elders to Church – all in black, and looking fearfully like a funeral without the body – under the escort of three Beadles.

'Think', said Francis, as he stood at the Inn window, admiring, of being taken to the sacred edifice by three Beadles! I have in my early time, been taken out of it by one Beadle; but, to be taken into it by three, O Thomas, is a distinction I shall never enjoy!'[6]

Then, unlike now, most of the streets of Lancaster, as Goodchild humorously observes, were extremely narrow – China Lane was a mere 8 feet wide. Then as now, however, the King's Arms Royal Hotel was strategically sited on the route to the Priory, the Castle (hardly a fragment of castle, surely?) and the railway station and no doubt, after a copious dinner and the satisfaction of an evening's writing, Dickens, like Goodchild, was happy to indulge in good-natured banter on the plain provincial piety of the church-goers of Lancaster as they trooped past his window on the Sunday morning to hear Bellew preach.

If not blacker and more pious than usual they were perhaps more numerous for not only was the Rev. John Chippendall Montesquieu Bellew (1823–74) one of the most dramatic pulpit orators of his day but he was born and had been educated in Lancaster. The son of Captain Robert Higgin and grandson of John Higgin, who was for many years governor of Lancaster Castle, he had assumed his mother's name for family legal reasons and gone from the Royal Grammar School to Oxford, from there to India and thence to London as assistant minister at St. Philip's, Regent Street, to become one of the most popular preachers in the capital. It was said of him that no pulpit orator of his time had greater natural gifts or had done more to cultivate them. He published several volumes of his sermons and, in 1863 a long novel, *Blount Tempest*, but in 1868 resigned his position and a sizeable income to become a convert to catholicism. He subsequently devoted his time to literature, composed and annotated a voluminous anthology of English poetry for students (1868), but more particularly became an extremely successful public reader, rivalling Fanny Kemble and Dickens himself.[7] In 1870 he created a sensation by the curious feat of reading *Hamlet* from the orchestra pit with actors miming the play behind him on stage. As happened with Dickens, these electrifying readings, which included two tours of the United States, overtaxed his strength and he died at the age of fifty-one.

At Lancaster this autumn weekend of 1857 he was thirty-four and at the height of his powers. Before preaching on the Sunday he had, on the Friday evening, delivered a public lecture on 'Palestine' in the Assembly Room. Described by the *Lancaster Guardian* of 19th September as a 'studious traveller' in the Holy Land and 'the most popular preacher of the Establishment in London' he 'met with a most hearty welcome from his townsmen' and the paper saw fit to reproduce the gist of his talk in four columns followed by a further two and a half columns the following week.[8] Nor did the paper fail to remind its readers under its 'Literary Notices' that Bellew's sermons could be purchased forthwith. *The Lancaster Gazette* of the same day carried an advertisement equally laudatory. Half a guinea was the price of each of two volumes, published by Boone & Co. of London and Thomas Edmondson of Lancaster, 'admirable not only as powerful inculcations of Divine Truth, but remarkable for beauty of composition as well as for the vein of elegant scholarship which runs through them'.[9]

Despite the landlord's remark Bellew appears not to have been a friend of Dickens, who refrained from following the crowd to hear him preach. Not that he would have been short of time to do so. Sunday railway timetables being what they are and were – 'Sabbath observance throws all the trains out', complained the writer to his sister-in-law – he had time to see the town and its surrounding area before catching a train for Leeds, en route for Doncaster, later that same day.[10] Collins was now managing to hobble about 'with two thick sticks, like an admiral in a farce'.[11] In *The Lazy Tour*, Goodchild, a more energetic character than Idle, (as Dickens was compared to Collins or indeed to most other people, and in any case Idle, faithful to his real-life model, has sprained his ankle) proceeds to 'explore the country from the top of all the steep hills in the neighbourhood', including in his investigations the local 'lunatic asylum' – 'an immense place . . . admirable offices, very good arrangements, very good attendants, altogether a remarkable place'.[12] The Moor Hospital as it is now known, begun in 1811 and opened in 1816, is in fact described at some length by Goodchild, and we know, from the *Lancaster Guardian* that the novelist did visit it, for the newspaper published the following short insert:

MR. CHARLES DICKENS: This eminent *Litterateur*, accompanied by Mr Wilkie Collins, the artist, who have been on a tour in the Lake District, arrived in this town on Saturday evening last from Carlisle and took up their quarters at the King's Arms. Several gentlemen of the town, on learning of the arrival of Mr. Dickens, left their cards at the hotel. On Sunday the two gentlemen, accompanied by the Rev. F. B. Danby, visited the asylum, and were shown through the principal departments of that well-conducted establishment, and made many enquiries as to its management. On the following day, the two gentlemen left for Doncaster.[13]

In *The Lazy Tour* Goodchild recounts to Idle, who did not accompany him (did the lame Collins really go along with Dickens, one wonders?) that he has seen

Long groves of blighted men-and-women-trees, interminable avenues of hopeless faces; numbers, without the slightest power of really combining for any earthly purpose; a society of human creatures who have nothing in common but that they have all lost the power of being humanly social with one another . . .

In one gallery . . . which looked to me about the length of the Long Walk, at Windsor . . . which was otherwise clear of patients (for they were all out), there was a poor little dark-chinned, meagre man with a perplexed brow and a pensive face, stooping low over the matting on the floor, and picking out with his thumb and forefinger the course of its fibres. The afternoon sun was slanting in at the large end-window, and there were cross patches of light and shade all down the vista, made by the unseen windows and the open doors of the little sleeping-cells on either side. In about the centre of the perspective, under an arch, regardless of the pleasant weather, regardless of the solitude, regardless of approaching footsteps, was the poor little dark-chinned, meagre man, poring over the matting . . . it came into my mind, that probably the course of those fibres as they plaited in and out, over and under, was the only course of things in the whole wide world that it was left to him to understand . . . Then, I wondered whether he looked into the matting, next, to see if it could show him anything of the process through which *he* came to be there, so strangely poring over it. Then I thought how all of us, God help us! in our different ways are poring over our bits of matting, blindly enough, and what confusions and mysteries we make in the pattern. I had a sadder fellow-feeling with the little dark-chinned, meagre man, by that time, and I came away.[14]

The almost cinematographic qualities of this passage, the way in which it is lit, staged and even choreographed are striking. It burns through the picaresque jocular fiction of *The Lazy Tour* with the intensity of starkly observed reality. In its eeriness it presages too the ghost story which is immediately to follow, but whereas *The Bride's Chamber* episode is a piece of atmospheric nonsense, the Moor Hospital incident discreetly points a number of chilling signals. The gaunt emptiness of the Moor gallery with its single perplexed occupant contrasts powerfully with the sumptuousness and conviviality of the 'good old Inn'. We are reminded of the polarisation of a society where, as Dickens pointed out in his description of the hotel, conspicuous wealth can have its source in secret 'slave-gain', where the sane and the efficient can exile the reminders of their own mental fragility in prisons on the town's periphery, there to be inspected by reverends and the occasional passing writer. Perhaps most remarkable however is the way in which Dickens sees the thin inmate of the Moor as representative of all men and not least of the novelist plaiting and weaving mysteries into a pattern. In the mirror-like mahogany of the old hotel the writer sees the slave; in the madman of the hospital he sees himself. This is Dickens at his must lucid and most human, the recorder of the realities of the great carcereal systems, the prisons, the workhouses, the Bedlams set up in the name of civilisation.

Idle, understandably, does not relish his friend's account of the Moor, and preferring talk of hunger to talk of insanity steers the conversation to grouse, custards and bride-cake and the two repair to dinner – 'an admirable performance', despite the cake being 'as bilious and indigestible as if a real Bride had cut it'.[15]

The two travellers are even more impressed by the atmosphere of the Lancaster hotel than by its food:

The house was a genuine old house of a very quaint description, teeming with old carvings, and beams, and panels, and having an excellent old staircase, with a gallery or upper staircase, cut off from it by a curious fence-work of old oak, or of the old Honduras mahogany wood. It was, and is, and will be for many a long year to come, a remarkably picturesque house; and a certain grave mystery lurking in the depth of the old mahogany panels, as if they were so many deep pools of dark water – such, indeed, as they had been much among when they were trees – gave it a very mysterious character after nightfall.

When Mr. Goodchild and Mr. Idle had first alighted at the door, and stepped into the sombre, handsome old hall they had been received by half a dozen noiseless old men in black, all dressed exactly alike, who glided upstairs with the obliging landlord and waiter – but without appearing to get into their way, or to mind whether they did or no – and who had filed off to the right or left on the old staircase, as the guests entered their sitting-room. It was then broad, bright day. But, Mr. Goodchild had said, when their door was shut: 'Who on earth are those old men?' And afterwards, both on going out and coming in, he had noticed that there were no old men to be seen.[16]

In short a hotel with an atmosphere and attendant figures fit to thicken the plot for the ghost-story that Idle-Collins and Goodchild-Dickens set about writing there and then, and which was to be located *in situ*.

In *The Bride's Chamber* episode of the story, the title and central feature of which are elaborated from the bride-cake that was served to the two writers, conversation is engaged with one of these mysterious old men supernaturally summoned by the stroke of one o'clock in the morning. On being asked by Goodchild whether condemned criminals are hanged at Lancaster Castle and whether their faces on the scaffold are turned towards the castle walls, the old man replies with some conviction:

'Your face is turned . . . to the Castle wall. When you are tied up, you see its stones expanding and contracting violently, and a similar expansion and contraction seem to take place in your own head and breast. Then, there is a rush of fire and an earthquake, and the Castle springs into the air, and you tumble down a precipice'[17]

He then proceeds to spin a bloodthirsty if somewhat laborious yarn of greed, murder and haunted chamber before finally revealing that he is himself none other than the ghost of the murderer whose tale he has told:

'His money could do nothing to save him, and he was hanged. I am he, and I was hanged at Lancaster Castle, with my face to the wall, a hundred years ago!'[18]

Joseph Sly, the owner and manager of the King's Arms was, however, no ghost, and though used to receiving notables in his 'excellent hotel' must have been more than pleased to welcome Charles Dickens.

'Accustomed as you are to the homage which men delight to render to the Inimitable' wrote Dickens to his sister-in-law (the Inimitable being himself), 'you would be scarcely prepared for the proportions it assumes in this northern country. Station masters assist him to alight from carriages, deputations await him in hotel entries, innkeepers bow down before him and put him into regal rooms'[19]

And Mine Host Sly it was, no doubt, who not only impressed Dickens with the hotel he ran but provided him with some of the background material on Lancaster that was put to use in *The Lazy Tour*. Sly must have later read the story with pleasure and presumably some pride and have written as much to Dickens, adding some personal remarks about his own life, for he received the following reply:

'Tavistock House'
London W.C.
Third December 1857

Sir,

I am sorry that I have until now, accidentally omitted to answer your letter.

I assure you that I received it with much pleasure. It was very agreeable to me to know that you were gratified by my having associated a little fancy with your excellent house; and I was particularly interested by your account of your honourable career in life.

I wish you every prosperity, and am

Faithfully Yours

Charles Dickens[20]

Sly was born in London on 12th December 1814 and had taken over the lease of the King's Arms in 1856 only a year before Dickens stayed there, having previously been proprietor of The Feathers Hotel in China Lane. unfortunately, unlike Dickens for whom he wrote one, we have no account of his career before that time, and Dickens destroyed most of the letters he received, Sly's being no exception. We do, however, know rather more about the unusual hotel managed and furnished by this unusual man.

The building was erected in 1625 as the town residence of Mr. Braddyll, a merchant who carried on a prosperous business with the Indies. In the Lancaster historian Cross Fleury's day – the last decades of the nineteenth century – there was a stone with the date 1625 underneath a third-storey window on the King Street side of the new hotel, but this is either no longer visible or has been removed, although high on the facade there is the inscription 'Established 1625. Rebuilt 1879'.(Figure 3.1) It was only in the latter half of the eighteenth century that the house became the King's Arms Hotel with the subsequent addition of the adjective *Royal*. Joseph Sly became proprietor on 12th May 1856 taking a twenty-one year lease. The inn, the most important one in the town, was a very large concern, with stabling for sixty-five horses and coach houses for seventy carriages. Before the Lancaster and Carlisle Railway opened in 1846 Lancaster was the terminus of the railway in the North-West and a thriving posting business centred on the hotel. After the railway was pushed further north this business declined, but in the middle of the front page of the *Lancaster Gazette* Sly regularly advertised his 'new and fashionable open and closed private carriages for hire' which, as well as to many others no doubt, were a boon to lame men of letters arriving at the station.[21]

The entrance hall of the hotel was spacious and grand, boasting a mahogany-cased clock (one of only three 'invented by Dr. Benjamin Franklin of Philadelphia' and the only one to be found in England).[22] Past the solid oak screen the 'uncommonly quaint' staircase that led from the hall and which so appealed to Dickens with its 'old Honduras mahogany' dated from Elizabethan times. (Figure 3.2) Several of the bedrooms were named after former occupants of distinction, the nameplates being displayed above the doors, as was the great saloon with its inscription 'Crowned Heads of Europe Room'. In it there hung what was claimed to be an original Gobelins tapestry from Paris, with a design by either Lebrun or Lesueur, depicting the combat of Achilles and Hector against a background of the city of Troy and valued, according to Cross Fleury, at £6500, though when sold at auction in 1877 it fetched 145 guineas. It was said of it that not only would the heir

THE OLD KING'S ARMS HOTEL, LANCASTER, MAY 1879.

Figure 3.1: Reproduced with the permission of Lancaster City Museum and Art Gallery.

ENTRANCE HALL AND ANCIENT STAIRCASE.

KING'S ARMS HOTEL, LANCASTER.

/1871

JOSEPH SLY, Proprietor.

Figure 3.2: Reproduced with the permission of Lancaster City Museum and Art Gallery.

apparent to the English throne have liked it for Sandringham but that the French Emperor Napoleon III had begun negotiations with Sly, through a gentleman, to buy it back for France, before the defeat of the Empire in the Franco-Prussian War put an end to the parleying. The room itself boasted its title from the various royal dignitaries who had put up or dined at the hotel 'since the peace' – the 1815 peace presumably – and amongst whom figured the Dowager Queen Adelaide, widow of William IV, who stayed on the night of 28 July 1840, Prince Louis Napoleon who breakfasted there on 6 December 1846, and the Grand Duke of Russia and his suite who made a stop there on 8 July 1847. Earlier, on 15 January 1837, Sir Robert Peel had slept a night *incognito* under the name of Jones. At a later date the Emperor and Empress of the Brazils spent a night in the hotel.[23]

Among the named bedrooms were the Lonsdale and Brougham Rooms, one with a four-poster bedstead dating from 1646. There was a similar carved antique bed in the room named after Lady Burdett-Coutts, the bank heiress and philanthropist, a close friend of Dickens who had banked with Coutts since 1837. Sly declined an offer of 250 guineas from the Lancaster and London firm of Gillow and Son acting for a client who wished to purchase this item. After September 1857, as might have been expected, there was also a Charles Dickens Room, fitted, amongst other furniture, with a 'massive four-post oak bedstead in the Norman style' of about 1540, a state chair in rich China silk and a three hundred years old sampler of embroidered silk depicting Old Testament scenes from the life of Abraham. When Dickens stayed there he noted that there were two red four-posters in the room. Interestingly the Abraham silk-work piece, measuring 21" long and 17" high, together with a second one hanging in the room, representing the 'budding of the tulip and the various stages of its growth' and decorated with peacock motifs (17" long by 14" high) have been described in some detail by Ruskin.

From his very early days in the 1830s Ruskin had stayed at the hotel with his parents on journeys north. In 1871 after a serious mental illness he had, without first seeing it, bought 'Brantwood' on Lake Coniston. It was to be his home to the end of his life. On 28 January 1873 he wrote to Lady Waterford:

> I have got a small cottage and a rock or two of my own, now, here – No other house for four miles south of me by the lake side – and few north of me – and I can walk for hours and meet nothing but sheep – which is very blessed to me after the foul tumult of London . . . no loveliness can exceed these lake and stream delightsomenesses.[24]

It was in September 1872 that the house was ready for him and he took possession of it. In his diary for Monday 11 September 1871, on his first journey to see 'Brantwood', he writes, after leaving Euston at 10.00 in the morning:

> Got to Lancaster past five. Walked up to castle, down by riverside (Lune). Rocks in sand on shore with gliding waters. Mr. Moore at tea. Mr. Sly's King's Arms.[25]

And the following day's entry reads:

> Before breakfast, up to moors, had view of castle and winding of Lune, very lovely. Mr. Sharpe at breakfast. To Furness Abbey, Coniston in evening. First visit to my house.[26]

His settling at 'Brantwood' increased the occasions he had for staying overnight at Lancaster and the diary records him there on 26 December 1872 en route from Oxford and again on 12 April 1875 on his way south. It was to the *Lancaster Observer* of 25 March 1887 that he wrote his famous letter fulminating against 'Railway Promoters'.

It so happens that 'Design in the Florentine School of Engraving', the sixth and last of his lectures on 'Wood and Metal Engraving', given in Oxford in December 1872 and collected in 1876 under the title of *Ariadne Florentina*, was revised by him in the same King's Arms and probably in the same room in which Dickens had written *The Bride's Chamber*. Into his lecture Ruskin incorporated a description of the silkwork embroidery.

> On the walls of the little room where I finally revise this lecture hangs an old silken sampler of great grandame's work: representing the domestic life of Abraham: chiefly the stories of Isaac and Ishmael. Sarah at her tent door, watching with folded arms the dismissal of Hagar: above, in a wilderness full of fruit trees, birds and butterflies, little Ishmael lying at the root of a tree, and the spent bottle under another; Hagar in prayer, and the panel appearing to her out of a wreathed line of gloomily undulating clouds, which, with a dark-rayed sun in the midst, surmount the entire composition in two arches, out of which descend shafts of (I suppose) beneficent rain; leaving, however, room, in the corner opposite to Ishmael's angel, for Isaac's, who stays Abraham in the sacrifice; the ram in the thicket, the squirrel in the plum tree above him, and the grapes, pears, apples, roses and daisies in the foreground, being all wrought with involution of such ingenious needle-work as may well rank, in the patience, the natural skill, and the innocent pleasure of it, with the truest works of Florentine engraving. Nay; the actual tradition of many of the forms of ancient art is in many places evident, – as, for instance in the spiral summits

of the flames of the wood on the altar, which are like a group of first-springing fern. On the wall opposite is a smaller composition, representing Justice with her balance and sword, standing between the sun and moon, with a background of pinks, borage and corncockle: a third is only a cluster of tulips and iris, with two Byzantine peacocks; but the spirits of Penelope and Ariadne reign vivid in all the work – and the richness of pleasurable fancy is as great still, in these silken labours, as in the marble arches and golden roof of the cathedrals of Monreale.[27]

Joseph Sly, as Cross Fleury said, 'was intensely proud of his ancient house, and sought to make it a museum as well as a comfortable home worthy of the highest patronage'.[28] With help from Capt. Coupland of the cabinet-maker and upholsterer firm of Bell and Coupland in Stonewell, and from Gillow & Co., Sly had stocked a treasure-house of antiques and curios. Contributing an account of his travels in the Lake District to the *New York Christian Intelligencer* of 12 August 1875, the Rev. E. P. Rogers wrote:

> It is worth a journey to the town to visit this same old Inn . . . a quaint old hostelry, with a carved staircase of the fifteenth century . . . filled with a rare collection of antiques in tapestry, paintings, plates, furniture and china. Here you may sleep, as one of our party did, in King James's bedstead, with the magnificent carving and the royal canopy above you; or you may occupy Lord Brougham's room or Dickens's; or if you are to be particularly honoured (and Americans generally are) you may even have the apartments designated over the door as those once occupied by the 'Crowned Heads of Europe'. We, being a modest party, were contented with the room once appropriated to 'H.R.H. Albert Edward, Prince of Wales'.[29]

The Spectator contended that

> Most of the things in the house are relics from battlefields; spoils of the strife of creeds, the strife of dynasties, the strife of fortune . . . The ancient furniture, the pride of the collection has been gathered from churches and castles and homesteads which are dust . . . The cabinets, the sideboards, the ancient wardrobe and the chairs – one is said to have belonged to King Henry VII and subsequently to have formed a portion of the effects of Queen Catherine Parr – were all curious and many of them were beautiful, but the beds and the chests were more interesting to a mere observer than any of the other objects.[30]

The World, a newspaper that had originated at a dinner in Bellew's London house, claimed that the inn housed 'the best collection of antique bedsteads in England.[31] With allowance made for hyperbole and legend the furniture and decoration of the hotel were manifestly as unusual and as sumptuous as the meals served there and of an equally stimulating taste.

Neither the furnishings nor the food of the 'good old Inn' were to be forgotten by Dickens who returned to Lancaster four years later, during the second series of his provincial reading tours, to give one of those dramatic performances that were to earn him in all about £45,000 but to cost him his health. On the evening of Thursday 12 December 1861 he gave two readings in the Music Hall – now the Grand Theatre – in St. Leonard Gate, selecting *Marley's Ghost* and *The Trial from Pickwick*, of which latter he was to give a total of one hundred and sixty-four readings up and down the country and abroad. Before the recital he had qualms about his Lancaster audience but they proved unwarranted. To W. H. Wills he wrote, 'Both Carlisle and Lancaster have come out admirably, though I doubted both as you did'.[32] *The Lancaster Gazette* wrote of the event that 'the reserve, notwithstanding the somewhat high charge, 4s. 0d. was an excellent one, the dress circle being well filled with the *elite* of the town and neighbourhood . . . the distinguished author of the readings was received with great applause'. On this occasion too Dickens put up at the old King's Arms and was visited there by the Mayor, Henry Gregson, and the Vicar, Canon Turner.[33] Some months afterwards his satisfaction with the creature comforts offered by Joseph Sly led him, whether spontaneously or by request is uncertain, to present the hotelier, now a friend, with a good-sized lithograph portrait of himself inscribed 'Monday 30th June 1862. Charles Dickens: to his good friend Mr. Sly'. (Figure 3.3) In a fine gilt frame this hung proudly in the great Elizabethan staircase of the inn. It is not known if the writer gave the portrait on a visit or had it sent from London, the latter seeming more probable.

Figure 3.3: R. J. Lane, Lithograph of Charles Dickens.

Reproduced with the permission of Lancaster City Museum and Art Gallery.

Some years later, in 1865, the novelist paid Sly the further compliment of a mention by name in chapter III of the story entitled *Dr. Marigold*, ascribing to his chief character, who tells of spending a couple of nights in the town before going on to Carlisle, the following snatch of dialogue:

'We were down at Lancaster, and I had done two nights more that fair average business (though I cannot in honour recommend them as a quick audience) in the open square there, near the end of the street where Mr. Sly's King's Arms & Royal Hotel stands'.[34]

Hardly flattering for Lancaster audiences (had they after all been so responsive at the reading in December 1861?) but a clear reference to the town's Market Square and resounding publicity for Joseph Sly who, the following Christmas, wishing to return the compliment, despatched a gift to London. This time Dickens was not slow in replying – on the small blue notepaper of the Athenaeum:

Dear Mr. Sly,

I am exceedingly obliged to Mrs. Sly and you for the noble box of game you have sent me, and for which I beg you, both, to accept my cordial thanks. It arrived in the best condition.

With all good wishes in and out of season, for the prosperity of your matchless and fine old house. Believe me always

Faithfully yours,

Charles Dickens[35]

Almost a year later it was the gift of the portrait that gave rise to the next letter from Dickens to the landlord:

Gad's Hill Place
Higham by Rochester, Kent
Friday 9th Nov. 1866

Dear Mr. Sly,

Dr. Hood, a friend of mine who stayed at your house last Friday, thought very highly of a portrait of myself that I gave you, and has written to ask me where the engraving can be got. I do not remember what portrait it is. Will you be so good as let me know whether there are any names – of painter, engraver, publisher or whatever – attached to it, and, if any, what the names are?

Faithfully yours,

Charles Dickens[36]

Sly presumably obliged with the information on the bottom of the portrait that it was drawn on stone by R. J. Lane A.R.A. from a photograph by John and Charles Watkins of Parliament Street. He followed up his letter a month later with a similar Christmas present to the last one and again Dickens wrote promptly to thank him

Gad's Hill Place,
Higham by Rochester, Kent.
Saturday. Twenty-second December

Dear Mr. Sly,

I beg to acknowledge with many thanks the safe receipt of your box of fine game, which arrived here in the very best condition.

With all the good wishes of the time, Believe me

(signature cut out by a collector)[37]

Joseph Sly was not slow to recognize the publicity he could gain for his business from his association with Dickens and from the references to the hotel that the writer had generously incorporated into his fiction. In the archives of Lancaster Museum there is a silk-bound booklet entitled *A Visit to Lancaster by Charles Dickens*, printed and published by G. C. Clark at the *Gazette* Office in 1866, describing the King's Arms and quoting the text of *Household Words* with extracts too from the *Official Illustrated Guide* of the Lancaster & Carlisle, Caledonian and Edinburgh and Glasgow Railways. A pamphlet in the same archives, published by same office, though without a date, contains much of the same material and is clearly a commercial publicity brochure version of the silk-bound presentation volume that must have been a prized family possession.[38] The British Library holds a virtually identical copy of the pamphlet, dated 1875.

During Christmas of 1867 Dickens was in America and so no box of Lancaster game was sent off by the munificent and grateful landlord but an 1868 offering brought a written response on Christmas Day:

> Gad's Hill Place
> Higham by Rochester, Kent.
> Christmas Day 1868

Dear Mr. Sly,

Your bounteous-filled box has arrived here safely today. With its contents in the best condition. Accept my cordial thanks and all good wishes of the season, both for yourself and to those around you, and for the rare old house in Lancaster.

Faithfully yours

Charles Dickens.[39]

On his Farewell Tour of readings Dickens again gave a recital in Lancaster on 31 March 1869 and later that year the by now customary present from the old King' Arms was as usual gratefully acknowledged:

> Gad's Hill Place,
> Higham by Rochester, Kent
> Thursday 16th December 1869

Dear Mr. Sly,

I have safely received your handsome present of game, in fine condition – all good Christmas wishes to you, and yours, and the rare old house.

With many thanks,

Faithfully yours.

Charles Dickens.[40]

It was to be the last Lancaster Christmas box received and acknowledged, for Dickens died, aged 58, in June of the following year 1870.

The 'matchless and fine old house', half hotel, half museum, that had so struck his imagination and appealed to his temperament, and which had inspired the writing of *The Bride's Chamber* ghost story, did not survive him for very long. Joseph Sly's twenty-one year lease on the property expired on 12 May 1877. He was sixty-two years old and decided to retire. In April the hotel was put up for lease again and the valuable collection of furniture, fittings and *objets d'art* auctioned off through the Preston valuers Holden and Whelan, Mr. John Burton 'the art connoisseur' of Preston conducting the proceedings. The sale, previously advertised far and wide in *The Spectator* and *The World*, amongst other publications, attracted widespread attention. It was held in the billiard room of the hotel on Wednesday and Thursday 11 April. Prefixed to the British Library copy of the publicity brochure are three handbills announcing the sale of the 'Valuable and Historical Contents', including portraits of the Stanley family attributed to Sir Godfrey Kneller and Sir Peter Lely. A fine catalogue was published to be had for the price of one shilling, and entitled *Catalogue of Rare Objects of Mediaeval Decorative*

Design and Stately Domestic Equipment: Substantial Monuments of Refined Taste and Handicraft of Olden Times.[41] The reading of it moved the *Lancaster Guardian* reporter to quote a particularly purple patch, describing the collections as: 'an aggregation of trophies unparalleled of their kind, the fruits of Mr. Sly's life-long love-chase, in which that gentleman's aesthetic proclivities have been plied with the assiduity of an instinctive connoisseur and a devotion that counted no cost.[42] *The Spectator*'s article, less bombastic, was tinged with nostalgia:

> Everything in the house looked as immovable as it was ancient. The walls and the door-frame bristled with brackets of old oak, which tell the tale of their derivation – here is a bishop's mitre, there a baron's escutcheon . . . It was a pleasant sight to see before the dispersion of it all and it was pleasant to leave it still undisturbed.[43]

The two-day sale of the 'Aesthetic Effects' raised the sum of £1840. The Franklin clock went to Mr Garnett of Quernmore Park, Lancaster, for £5 10s. 0d., the fifteenth-century Derby state bedstead for £80 to Capt. Coupland, who was buying, amongst other clients, for the Duke of Norfolk. The tapestries and samplers, grandly described as 'Goodly Arras of Great Majestie', were dispersed – the Gobelins *Combat of Achilles and Hector* was sold for 145 guineas to Mr. Harris of Lancaster 'amidst applause'. The work depicting Diana and Acteon, Perseus and Andromeda fell to Mr. Royd for 12 guineas. The Abraham piece, the Tulip and Peacock piece and the work representing Justice with Balance and Sword – all three described by Ruskin – went to Mr. Bell of the Royal Exchange, Manchester, for 11 guineas, 12 guineas and £13 10s. 0d. respectively. Where are they, one wonders, now? A complete set of Hogarth's *Mariage à la Mode* fetched 12 guineas.[44] The signed portrait of Dickens escaped the hammer. With the letters from the novelist it was kept in the Sly family, the letters being subsequently donated, in 1948, by the landlord's grandson, Joseph Sly (1881–1952) of Morecambe, to the Lancaster Public Library and the portrait to the Lancaster Museum. By then the letters had already been published, in 1929, in Thomas Cann Hughes's *Literary Associations of Lancaster and District*.[45]

The hotel itself was taken over by Samuel Ducksbury. Two years later in 1879 he had the entire building demolished and the present commercial hotel of the same name erected on the site. Of the Elizabethan house with its staircase, mahogany panels, bride-cake and mysterious old men nothing remained. The motives for its destruction are open to surmise. Were they solely commercial? The success and the glamour that had attached themselves to Joseph Sly's enterprise must have caused resentment amongst certain circles, not least fellow hoteliers of the town.

With the 'rare old house' and its antique furniture gone, Joseph Sly, remembered as 'good-natured, plump and cherubic', lived in semi-retirement spending some of the year in Lancaster but the summers at 'Tower Wood', his home on Windermere, between Lakeside and Bowness. He enjoyed trips on the lake in his steamlaunch 'Sunbeam' and built a boathouse that was compared to a mini-castle. It seems he was a man of substantial means. On 22 August 1895 he died of 'congestive apoplexy' at the age of eighty. He was buried in Lancaster Cemetery on Saturday 24 August alongside his wife Elizabeth (21.2.1818 – 11.11.1883) who had predeceased him and who was doubtless the unsung creator of the bride-cake that inspired Dickens to his story and of many another comfort in her husband's hotel. A full column obituary was published in the *Lancaster Observer* of 23 August 1895.

Half a century later the City of Lancaster had occasion to officially remember Joseph Sly. In 1947 his grandson, Joseph Sly of Morecambe, who shortly afterwards also donated the Dickens portrait and letters, presented back to the city a silver epergne which the town itself had given to his grandfather in recognition of a special service.

On 10 March 1863, the year after Dickens had given his portrait to Sly, the Prince of Wales was to be married to Princess Alexandra. Landlord Joseph Sly felt that Lancaster should mark the occasion in an original manner. Food and festivities, not to speak of the 'Crowned Heads of Europe' were his forte. He devised and organised, with his innate theatrical flair, a grand grotesque torchlight procession through the town on the eve of the wedding. The pageant included 'Two Salamanders in Fire-Brigade Accoutrements, Sir Plum Pudding Bart., attended by his Chaplain, Sir Loin Beef, Mr. Punch mounted on a full-bred Jerusalem pony, etc.'. The event was recorded in a remarkable water-colour painting – now in Lancaster Museum – by Alice Quarme (1827-1892), the Lancaster artist, daughter of Charles Edward Quarme (1795–1879) former owner of the *Lancaster Gazette*. Popular prints depicting the occasion were also made.[46] Two whole oxen were obtained by subscription, for distribution to the poor. They were roasted in public together with eight rounds of beef and one thousand pounds of 'rich plum pudding'. The cooking was superintended, throughout the night, by Mrs. Sly. With cheese and 'home-brewed', a feast for two thousand persons was held in the New Market at 10.00 on the wedding morning. Pageant and feast, which 'exceeded any held out of the metropolis' were a spectacular success.

These 1863 festivities were not Sly's only gastronomic homage to the Royal Family. Four years later he organised a more personal event. On Saturday 2 November 1867 Queen Victoria, on a rail journey south from Scotland, breakfasted at 9 o'clock at the Castle Station. Catering was by courtesy of Sly. The menu, printed on fringed white silk, stretched to five courses, including Galantine of Turkey, Partridges in Aspic, Cold Lobster, Broiled Kidneys and Preserved Magnum Bonum Plums, the meal being rounded off with the compulsory . . . bride-cake. Unlike Wilkie Collins Victoria did not need to worry about the cost. Mine Host Joseph Sly was, after all, not a man to have it said that his King's Arms had failed to delight his Queen's palate.

But it was to commemorate Joseph and Elizabeth Sly's gargantuan labours of 1864 'in high appreciation of their unwearied zeal and energy' that, on the original suggestions of the High Sheriff, W. A. F. Saunders of Wennington Hall, they were presented by the town with the solid silver epergne made by Elkington and Co. of Liverpool. One of the panels depicted a scene from the Carnival procession. The presentation was made on 9 November 1863 in the Upper Assembly Room in King Street. An account of it was included, naturally, in Sly's hotel publicity brochure.

By 1947, when the epergne was presented back to Lancaster, seventy years or so had passed since the razing of the hotel. Joseph Sly, impresario and collector *extraordinaire*, friend and correspondent of Charles Dickens, host of Ruskin, was long gone, along with his old King's Arms. Epergne, publicity brochure, portrait, a handful of documents, seven letters from Charles Dickens and, of course, *The Lazy Tour of Two Idle Apprentices* and *Dr. Marigold* remain sole testimony to a rare old hotel and its remarkable landlord.

Notes

An earlier version of this article was published with illustrations in *Comment* (Lancaster University Independent Staff-Student Magazine) Nos. 87 and 88, 13 Oct. and 16. Nov. 1978, 3–6 and 10–15. The author would be grateful for further information on the subject that readers might have, especially the whereabouts of art objects once belonging to Joseph Sly.

My thanks go to Lancaster City Museum and to Lancaster Public Library (in both of which there are Sly files) for the courteous co-operation of their staff, to Professor Kathleen Tillotson for ready advice and to Mr. Christopher Dickens and Mr. Graham Storey for kind permission to republish the Dickens letters.

1. Letter to Wilkie Collins, 29 Aug. 1857 in *Selected Letters of Charles Dickens*, edited by D. Paroissien, (London, 1985), p. 120.
2. Letter to John Forster, quoted in N. Page, *A Charles Dickens Companion* (London, 1984), p. 305.
3. Letter to Georgina Hogarth, 9 Sept. 1857 in *Letters of Charles Dickens*, 2 vols. (London, 1880), II, 30.
4. Signed holograph letter. This and the six subsequent letters from Dickens to Sly are in the archives of Lancaster Public Library catalogued at MS 5060–5066.
5. Letter to Georgina Hogarth, 12 Sept. 1857 in *Letters* (1880), II, 121.
6. *The Lazy Tour of Two Idle Apprentices* in *Christmas Stories*, (Oxford, 1956), p. 721 ff.
7. See *The Terrific Kemble*: Fanny Kemble, edited by Eleanor Ransome, (London, 1978).
8. *Lancaster Guardian*, 19 Sept. 1857, pp. 3–4 and 26 Sept. 1857, pp. 3–4.
9. *Lancaster Gazette*, 19 Sept. 1857, p. 4
10. Letter to Georgina Hogarth, 12 Sept. 1857 in *Letters* (1880), II, 31.
11. *Ibid.*
12. *The Lazy Tour*, p. 723.
13. *Lancaster Guardian*, 19 Sept. 1857, p. 5. The Rev. Francis Burton Danby, M.A., then aged 44, was Chaplain of the County Asylum after being Chaplain of Kendal House of Correction from 1844.
14. *The Lazy Tour*, pp. 723–25.
15. *Ibid.*, p. 725.
16. *Ibid.*, p. 725.
17. *Ibid.*, p. 727.
18. *Ibid.*, p. 737.
19. Letter to Georgina Hogarth, 12 Sept. 1857 in *Letters* (1880), II, 31.
20. Signed holograph letter MS 5061
21. Cross Fleury (Robert E. K. Rigbye), *Time-Honoured Lancaster*, (Lancaster, 1891); see *Lancaster Gazette* p. 1 during 1860s.
22. Publicity brochure and handbills of the sale held on 17 April 1877 catalogued under 'Joseph Sly', Brit. Lib. 8 10347 cc2 1–19 vol. Tracts 1826–1878.
23. Old King's Arms in *Lancaster Records* or *Leaves from Local History 1801–1850*, (Lancaster, 1869), G. C. Clark, *Gazette* Office.
24. *Sublime and Instructive*. Letters from John Ruskin to Louisa, Marchioness of Waterford, Anne Blunden and Ellen Heaton, ed. by Virginia Surtees, (London, 1972), p. 74.
25. *The Diaries of John Ruskin*, 3 vols., edited by Evans and Whitehouse, (Oxford, 1958) II, 711; Mr. Sharpe is the Lancaster architect Edmund Sharpe (1809–1877); Mr. Moore is unidentified.
26. *Ibid.*, II, 734, III, 841. In the mid 1870s Ruskin was on terms of friendship with a Mr. Joseph Sly and his wife, who ran the Waterhead Inn at Coniston. Joseph Sly of the old King's Arms had an elder son also named Joseph, born in 1842. I have not been able to establish whether Ruskin's Waterhead friend was the elder son or some other relation of Joseph Sly of Lancaster.
27. *The Works of Ruskin*, (Library Ed.) XXII, 452–53.
28. Cross Fleury, p. 452.
29. Bill of sale – see note 22 above.

30. *The Spectator*, April 1877, quoted in *Lancaster Observer*, 2 August 1895.
31. *The World*, 13 Sept. 1876.
32. Letter to W. H. Wills, 13 Dec. 1861 in *Letters*, (1880), II, 167.
33. *Lancaster Gazette*, 14 Dec. 1861, p. 5, and for an insert advertising the reading 7 Dec. 1861, p. 1.
34. *Dr. Marigold* (or *Dr. Marigold's Prescriptions*) in *Christmas Stories*, (Oxford, 1959), pp. 467–68.
35. Signed holograph letter. MS 5062.
36. Signed holograph letter. MS 5063. Dr. Hood might be Thomas Hood the younger (1835–1874), the poet and humorist who was a friend of Dickens, but could be Edwin Paxton Hood (1820–1885), a nonconformist cleric who worked for social reform and was a prolific author of popular fiction.
37. Holograph letter. MS 5064.
38. Entitled *Sly's King's Arms Lancaster. Extracts from Household Words* Relating to Mr. Charles Dickens's visit to Lancaster.
39. Signed holograph letter. MS 5065.
40. Signed holograph letter. MS 5066.
41. Catalogue in the Lancaster Museum Sly File.
42. *Lancaster Guardian*, 14 April 1877, p. 4, col.1.
43. See note 30 above.
44. *Lancaster Guardian*, 14 April 1877, p. 4, cols. 1 and 2.
45. Thomas Cann Hughes, *The Literary Associations of the County Town of Lancaster and its Surrounding Districts*, (Lancaster, 1929), pp. 38–40; the letters were also published in *The Letters of Charles Dickens*, 3 vols. 1938, Nonesuch Press, vols. II and III.
46. Details of the pageant in the silk-bound booklet in Lancaster Museum.

Chapter Four

Mrs Humphry Ward and the Great Houses of Westmorland: Levens Hall and Sizergh Castle

Alison Milbank

Although no less than three of Mary Ward's novels are currently in print – *Robert Elsmere* (1888), *Marcella* (1894) and *Helbeck of Bannisdale* (1898) – it is difficult for the modern reader to realise the extent of the fame and prestige she once enjoyed. Her novel of clerical loss of faith, *Robert Elsmere*, sold over a million copies in English by 1909, was translated into numerous other languages, and created a national debate. It was even suggested that the question, 'What do you think of Robert Elsmere?', be included in the 1890 census. Perhaps Mary Ward is best remembered today as the preternaturally solemn child in pigtails, in Max Beerbohm's cartoon, who interrogates a nonchalantly elegant Matthew Arnold, 'Why, Uncle Matthew, Oh why, will not you be always wholly serious?' (Figure 4.1), or as the 'Great Mary' of Ezra Pound who represented to a whole younger generation all that was most reactionary and self-complacent about the Victorians.[1]

This article will do little to question the picture of Mary Augusta Ward (1851–1920) as a social – and, indeed, an intellectual – conservative. The success of *Robert Elsmere*, like that of John Robinson's *Honest to God* in the 1960's, was partly due to its popularization of the religious debates of a previous, not the present generation. However, in her treatment of sexual passion Mary Ward is closer to Hardy and Lawrence than to the 'Eminent Victorians'. By attending to Ward's individual use of the geography and the buildings of Westmorland, and to her immersion in the life and works of the Brontës, I hope to show how this most unfeminist of writers (leader of the anti-suffrage league) dramatises questions of power and patriarchy, especially through the medium of theological discourse, with surprising freedom and directness.

By birth, Mary Ward was an Arnold, and a granddaughter of Dr Thomas Arnold of Rugby. At the age of seven, when her father returned from Tasmania, after his conversion to Roman Catholicism, she was sent to live with her Arnold aunts at Fox How, the house built by Dr Arnold, in local style and to Wordsworth's approval, at Rydal, at the foot of Loughrigg. In 'Sunday morning in Rugby Chapel', Mary's uncle, the poet and critic, Matthew Arnold, wrote of life with his father as being 'Rested as under the boughs of a mighty oak', and although Thomas Arnold had been long dead, the Arnold broad-church tradition, and the family's sense of its own worth provided security and shelter to Arnold's granddaughter, both then, and during all the crises of her immediate family history, her father's conversions and their accompanying poverty, and her parents' separation.

At Fox How, Mary Arnold was taken to tea with Wordsworth's widow; Harriet Martineau, the political economist and novelist, was a neighbour; Mrs Gaskell often stayed nearby; and, of course, Uncle Matthew often came to stay. So she was able to feel herself part of a wider literary and intellectual community, which sense helped to give her confidence when entering society at Oxford, where Tom Arnold, her father, gained a tutorship after his 'unconversion' in 1865. In *Milly and Olly, Or a Holiday among the Mountains* (1881) Mary Ward looked back at her childhood at Fox How, as if to the golden age, and she wrote of the house and its toys and traditions as if they had existed for centuries, and not a mere twenty years. This perspective is common to the perception of many a child, but it is clear that Mary Ward was particularly anxious to maintain a sense of continuity

Mr. Matthew Arnold. To him, Miss Mary Augusta, his niece: "Why, Uncle Matthew, Oh why, will not you be always wholly ..... ?"

Figure 4.1: Max Beerbohm, from his *The Poet's Corner*, 1904.

with a secure and stable past. The old house would, in many of her later novels, perfectly express this yearning for stability.

Fox How proved to be but a temporary refuge, since in 1858 Mary was sent to school at Eller How in Ambleside, where, as William Peterson has discovered, she performed such feats of defiance as breaking the panel of a door with her fists when immured inside as a punishment, and running 'up to the top of a flight of stairs with a large plate of bread-and-butter and flinging slice after slice smack in the face of the governess standing at the foot'.[2] Mary was miserable at all the various schools she was sent to, especially because she was sometimes a charity pupil and made to feel the humiliation of her position. Although she was, at one time, pupil of a school at Ambleside run by the great Jemima Clough, a famous educationalist who went on to be first principal of Newnham College, Cambridge, Mary Ward was quick to associate her childhood experience with that of Charlotte Brontë at Cowan Bridge. Fox How took on the allegorical meaning of Moor House in *Jane Eyre* where Jane finds shelter as a wanderer, and later a family. Mary Ward went on to edit the Haworth edition of the Brontës, and to argue (against her friend Henry James who wished to attempt some separation between the lives and literary productions) of the Brontë sisters and interpretation of their literary productions, that the life of Charlotte Brontë was what gave a book like *Jane Eyre* 'its genius'.[3] Ward was drawn both by the intimate and stimulating life of the little household at Haworth, and also by the isolated and orphaned status of Charlotte Brontë's heroines.

In *Robert Elsmere* Mary Ward recreates a Brontëan household of cultivated sisters in the isolated Westmorland valley of Longsleddale, north of Burneside, which she renames 'Long Whindale'. Their house is, like Fox How, the dwelling of incomers, and shows evidence of 'the sense of a changing social order'.(Mrs Humphry Ward's imperialism is shown here. The incursion of outsiders is always benign, bringing civilization, higher ethical values and culture to a somewhat depraved native stock.) The gentrified garden has lost 'the old-fashioned medley of phloxes, lavender bushes . . . and pampas grass' to be 'trimly laid with turf, dotted with neat flowerbeds'. No longer a working farm, 'curtains of some soft outlandish make showed themselves in what had once been a stable' (Chapter 1).[4] The sound of a violin echoes round the valley, and within the newly converted farm live three southern young women. This feminized dwelling provides the hero with a wife, but one who resembles the wild and stern valley rather than the aesthetic elegance of the little house. Catherine Leyburn has a Wordsworthian mystical simplicity, but all the protestant severity of the fells, to which her face is actually compared: 'About face and figure there was a delicate austere charm, something which harmonised with the bare stretches and lonely craggs of the fells' (Chapter 1).

But where Emily Brontë might write of affinity with the moors as a Romantic, in terms of physical and mental independence, Mary Ward presents Catherine as a 'true daughter of the mountains' because she shares their gentleness and severity. Like them she is out of time, and almost rigidified. Catherine remains sternly orthodox and reproving of her husband's religious doubts, which she regards as morally reprehensible. Indeed, her own steely sense of moral responsibility would have prevented her from marrying the man she undoubtedly loved, had it not been for another, equally forceful physical reality, the rain, which allows Elsmere to carry her across a swollen river, and to 'melt' her. It takes a rainstorm and flooding finally to 'dissolve' the 'Westmoreland strength' of her opposition (Chapter 8). Ward uses stone and water with the same metaphoric intensity and allegorical purpose that characterizes Charlotte Brontë's use of snow and fire in *Jane Eyre*.

In Mary Ward, the allegorical romance form that Charlotte Brontë evolved is adapted for the purposes of a novel of ideas, and it is, perhaps, this indirect relation to the Gothic and the allegorical Bunyanesque pilgrimage that renders Ward's novels so old-fashioned. In this tradition houses are as symbolically weighted as landscapes, weather and characters. If the Leyburns' farmhouse is the pastoral and familial retreat of the equally aquatically named Rivers family in *Jane Eyre*, the other significant house in *Robert Elsmere*, Murewell, resembles Thornfield, in so far as its Jacobean splendour and antiquity provides a scene both of attraction and temptation for the protagonist, who loses his faith through study of the contents of its library. Murewell is of the size and consequence of Knole in Kent, and it is typical of Mary Ward that the richness of its tradition is used to distance orthodox Christianity and the 'New Brotherhood' of dogmaless religion that Robert Elsmere goes on to found. The new faith is thereby proved to be but the natural heir of what went before, of Renaissance culture even.

Ward is aware, like George Eliot before her in *Romola* (1863), of the great historical divide between past and present, and the impossibility of ever satisfactorily closing the circle of interpretation. Her hero and Wendover, squire of Murewell, intend to write a history of 'Testimony' (reliable evidence for Biblical events), worried as they are about the lack of eyewitness corroboration of Christ's miracles. The great house of Murewell

Figure 4.2: Thomas Allom, *Interior of Sizergh Hall, Westmorland*, from his *Picturesque Rambles in Westmorland, Cumberland, Durham and Northumberland*, 1847.

is the appropriate place for such a study, in Ward's eyes, for it provides both a testimony to the past, and in its very existence it relates past to present. Ward seems even to view the Church of England in this light, as an ancient and ruinous mansion that all must help to prop up because of its vital historical testimony to the thoughts and beliefs of past generations, not because of its witness to present truth.

For her own part, Mary Ward sought always, after her marriage and first fashionably arts-and-crafts Morris and Co. furnishings in North Oxford, to inhabit old houses:

> If one may covet anything I think one may covet this kind of inheritance from the past to shelter one's own later life in. Life seems so short to make anything quite fresh in.[5]

The word 'shelter' returns us to Ward's desire for the security of the home and its tradition, a home both in terms of providing a physical shelter, but also here a 'place' in history.

While finally, on the proceeds of her vast sales, settling down to manorial life on a small country estate, Stocks, near Tring, Mary Ward transported her family to various rented summer homes of even grander style. Wordsworth's house, Rydal Mount, was once taken, and her daughter Dorothy pleased her mother by sighting the ghost of Wordsworth sitting on the window-seat in the room where his sister Dorothy died. In the summer of 1897, the Wards came to Levens Hall, the part-medieval, pele-towered seat of the Bagot family, situated on the River Kent, south of Kendal. The extreme antiquity of the place was a great attraction (the hall and tower date from the thirteenth century), but it was very cold, and some time had to be taken to establish a really cosy sitting-room in which Mary Ward could work. The romantic aura of Levens was to provide Mary Ward with a fictional setting as specific and figuratively rich as Longsleddale in *Robert Elsmere*.

Figure 4.3: Thomas Allom, *Levins Hall, Westmorland*, from his *Picturesque Rambles in Westmorland, Cumberland, Durham and Northumberland*, 1847.

While the Wards were at Levens, Mary Ward's father, now a Catholic professor in Dublin, came to stay, and the presence of a Catholic in the old house perhaps suggested the plot of *Helbeck of Bannisdale*, although the idea of a Catholic novel had been mooted the year before, when Mary Ward wrote to Tom Arnold:

> Would you mind my dearest, if I chose a certain Catholic background for my next story? I won't do it if you dislike it, but though of course my point of view is anything but Catholic, I should certainly do what I had thought of doing, with sympathy, & probably in such a way as to make the big English public understand more of Catholicism than they do now.[6]

While Levens Hall itself was not a Catholic house (although one of its former owners had Jacobite sympathies), it was in an area full of recusant families, and Sizergh Castle, equally ancient and pele-towered, only a mile or two distant, was a Catholic house. (Figure 4.2) The Stricklands had followed the Stuarts to France, and Lady Strickland had acted as governess to the young pretender. The case of relics over which Laura Fountain pored at Bannisdale (and which may still be seen by the visitor to Sizergh) must have been viewed by Mary Ward at Sizergh, not Levens. Mary Ward combines the mystique of these neighbouring houses, taking the history of Sizergh to the building of Levens. Both are grey stone border houses, centred on hall and tower, but, although Sizergh guards its family religious tradition within a wood-panelled, ancient castle, with over-mantles to rival the riches of Levens, its immediate surroundings of Victorian rock-garden cast a less gothic shadow than Levens, which is backed by a very early topiary garden of fantastic, vaguely allegorical and alchemical shapes. (Figure 4.3) Two women, Catherine,

Countess of Suffolk and Berkshire (d.1762), and Mary Howard (d.1877) held Levens in their own right, and one owner, Lady Andover (d.1803), lived at Levens many years as a widow. The filially loyal and conservative taste of these women ensured that little change was made to the house during the eighteenth and nineteenth centuries, and its ancient character remained untouched by modernization. But while the reader can 'place' whole scenes of the novel in specific Levens locations – the window recess in the drawing-room, the bowling green, the dining-room with its leather panelling – Mary Ward provides the house with an invented romantic history. She also provides her father's conversion to a new religion with the trappings of romance and tradition. In the two protagonists – Alan Helbeck, the Catholic owner of Bannisdale, and Laura Fountain, daughter of an agnostic Cambridge don – Mary Ward's father and the Arnoldian broad-church meet, and Ward attempts some reconciliation between these two inheritances.

What might surprise the reader who knows only *Robert Elsmere* is that the play of opposing thought-systems in Helbeck takes the form of a love story, and one, moreover, which does not merely clothe ideas in human garb. Difference of opinion, and fascination of the 'other' creates sexual attraction between the protagonists, and the whole discourse of conversion runs alongside a very real struggle for dominance.

As in traditional romance, man and woman begin by being cast, with ideological purity, as representatives of culture and nature respectively. Alan Helbeck shares the character of his house. Just as 'the whole structure seemed to lean upon and draw towards the tower, so the little household and the local catholic community shelter under his protection : tall, thin and austere, Helbeck is the tower 'which gave accent to a general expression of austerity' to the house. His extreme reserve is imitated by the way in which his house (unlike the real Levens) 'seemed to withdraw itself as into the rock "whence it was hewn" ' (Chapter 1).

By embowering Bannisdale in trees, and by setting it directly under a craggy fell, Mary Ward seeks to increase its evolutionary tie with the natural world around it. Like the Catholicism practised within its walls, it is omnivorous: everything, all meanings, must be drawn into its symbol-making life.

As the heroine penetrates the recesses of this grey house, she finds its owner a thoroughly Brontësque, tyrannical hero. His grand house with its (here, surprisingly) generous fires, and his erotic discourse of possession are reminiscent of Rochester in *Jane Eyre* (1847), although his austere beauty and extreme piety are the characteristics of St John Rivers in that same novel. His poverty and isolation, and the brooding way in which he sits silent in his carved chair of Westmorland oak in the ancient hall recall Heathcliff, whereas his great eyes and extreme delicacy, his good works, as well as a certain Catholic prurience are the marks of Paul Emmanuel, Lucy Snowe's Catholic lover, in *Villette* (1853).

What Mary Ward chooses to emphasise in this romantic stereotype is Helbeck's aristocratic birth and behaviour. This sense of long breeding, of Helbeck as the refined product of a tradition, is both intellectually important, enabling him to enjoy the same communion with the house that the house, as a building, enjoys with its own history, and religiously significant, because, through the mass, which Ward presents as a social activity, 'communion' is literally established between past and present, the dead and the living. A third use of Helbeck's aristocratic blood is to justify his seigneurial right to impose his will on that of Laura. Indeed, his delicacy towards her, his very refusal to ask her to act as he wishes, is only the sheathing of a power made all the more threatening by its reserve. To Laura, at first, this aristocratic air occasions joking remarks about the Vandyke portrait of Charles I, but soon she can quote Marvell's words about Charles 'He nothing common did or mean . . . '. The poem ('An Horation Ode upon Cromwell's Return from Ireland') describes Charles I's behaviour at his death, and this casts Helbeck as a victim, but Laura finds herself haunted by both house and Helbeck: 'Again and again the grey gabled mass thrust itself upon her attention, recalling each time, against her will, the face of its owner' (Chapter 4).

The house as a field of force, tyrannically imposing the will of its male owner upon a female captive, is the stuff of the Gothic, and Mary Ward is not afraid to exploit all the popular motifs: ancient ruined house, threat of sexual penetration, Roman Catholicism as tyranny and inquisition, the pull of an anachronistic past order on the present, and so on. Where Mary Ward is original, is in the way she transports the machinery of Roman Catholic authority from seventeenth-century Spain or Italy to an English country house. Moreover, the Catholicism described is a native current, the shared history of every pre-Reformation house or church in the country, only grown strange and old-fashioned by its imperviousness to changing fashions and beliefs in society at large. Here, the out-of-time quality of Catherine Leyburn's isolated Westmorland valley, and Helbeck's Westmorland mansion, have a similar function. Indeed, they are both composed of stone, resistant to change, only worn away, over time, by the action of water (and their watery surnames suggest the potential for each so to be altered).

Laura Fountain, as her two names suggest, bears the weight of the natural world within the novel. She is, indeed, descended, on her father's side, from Westmorland yeomen, so that, in Romantic ecstasy among the Brigsteer woods (north of Sizergh) at daffodil time, she can address the landscape itself as a parent: 'I am not a stranger – draw me to you – my life sprang from yours' (Chapter 3). This combination of religious agnosticism and nature mysticism invites comparison with pagan nymphs, and her room at Bannisdale shows a tapestry of Diana hunting in a forest, with a ship at sail nearby on a sea, 'windy enough for thoughts of love and flight'. While the tapestry speaks of the maiden freedom of the goddess, the presence of the ship reminds one of the need of the virgin to escape the pursuit of the male. So, for example, Laura runs out of Bannisdale one May night, to meet her infatuated cousin, Mason, in the park (following a path high above the river, which can still be followed, between oaks set out by Beaumont in the seventeenth century), in a landscape of pastoral eroticism:

> Even in this dim light the trees had the May magnificence – all but the oaks, which still dreamed of a best to come. Here and there a few tufts of primroses, on the bosom of the crag above the river, lonely and self-sufficing, like all loveliest things, starred the dimness of the rock. Laura's feet danced beneath her; the evening beauty and her passionate response flowed as it were into each other, made one beating pulse; never, in spite of qualms and angers, had she been more physically happy, more alive. (Book II, Chapter 2)

Laura then meets her cousin, who, maladroitly, asks for one of the *artificial* buttercups on her hat. His desire for this token reveals the hopelessness of his love, for Laura herself is as 'self-sufficing' in her intensity of response to the beauty around her as the wild flowers on the crag. It is her 'wild fearlessness' that prevents Mason from attempting, as he desires, to ravish her: 'to throw his powerful arms around her and keep her there, or carry her across the bridge – at his pleasure'.

It is interesting that here Ward reverses the set of associations, common enough in Hardy and Lawrence, whereby the house and civilisation are equated with the repressions and rules of social convention, and nature with spontaneous sexual congress and freedom. Nature, in the person of Laura Fountain, is certainly free and spontaneous, but it is also virginal – the Daphne who is turned into a laurel to elude her pursuer. The great house, and the person of Helbeck are together the huntsman, as Helbeck himself admits: 'It is her wild pagan self that I love – that I desire', and 'How she loathes all that we love – humility, patience, obedience! She would sooner die than obey. Unless she loved! Then what an art, what an enchantment to command her!' (Book II, Chapter 3).

What makes the language above unique is the particular admixture of sex and religion. Helbeck is both the lover and the priest – indeed, the chains of association linking him to his private chapel, in which heart imagery is used for both man and room, make him some sort of Christ figure, resembling the statue of the Sacred heart of Jesus, a devotion central to Catholic piety of the nineteenth century. It is Helbeck's heart that Laura kisses incessantly and hysterically at the point when she decides she must leave him. And Helbeck's own heart is within the house, enclosed further, within the chapel:

> But when Mr Helbeck is at home, the place becomes, as it were, the strong heart of the house. It beats through the whole organism; so that no-one can ignore or forget it. (Book III, Chapter 1)

Hence arises Laura's timidity about entering the chapel during her early days at Bannisdale, since to enter, and join its worship would be to yield herself, body and soul alike, to Helbeck's heart. When Laura does attend prayers, as Helbeck's affianced bride, 'she seemed to feel her whole self breaking up, dissolving in the grip of a power that was at once her foe, and the bearer of infinite seduction' (Book IV, Chapter 3). Here, sex is not the sub-text of a religious discourse, nor religion simply providing a language for a love-affair. Rather, both erotic and theological discourses provide a means to interrogate the manner in which patriarchy exercises its power.

As in the Gothic novels of Ann Radcliffe, and in the later romances of the Brontës, the isolated great house, precisely because of its separation from the world of the present time, and its complete loss of influence on the public world outside its gates, concentrates on imposing its will on its domestic inhabitants. As a result of being so apart, of having lost public power, its own life becomes eccentric, as Ward illustrates in her description of the topiary garden at Bannisdale:

> The garden was old and dark, like the Tudor house that stood between it and the sun. Rows of fantastic shapes carved in living yew and box stood ranged along the straight walks . . . At this time of year there were no flowers in the stiff flowerbeds . . . Only upon the high stone walls that begirt this strange and melancholy pleasure-ground, and in the 'wilderness' that lay on its eastern side between the garden and the fell, were Nature and Spring allowed to show themselves . . . Otherwise all was dark, tortured, fantastic, a monument of old-world caprice that the heart could not love, though piety might not destroy it. (Chapter 6)

In this dark view of it, the garden has the denial of natural growth that Ward attributes to Catholic asceticism and other-worldliness, in the way that plants are forced into artificial shapes, and light is filtered through the medium of the house, as grace is to the Catholic through the Church, not, as to the protestant, directly from God to the soul. 'Tortured' suggests both the horrific martyrdoms of the saints, and the sense of strain by which a faith carries on beyond its natural time. (Mary Ward is a follower of Carlyle in her view of belief systems as garments, to be shed when they are worn out).

In later scenes, the garden proves the site of revelations of the shadow-side of Catholic obedience. In the yew arbour, Laura is told by a Catholic cripple child the tale of a saint who forbore to visit a dying brother as an act of obedience to his superior; she is shown a disgusting relic of John of the Cross's finger beside the beech hedge. With its mazelike structure this garden is the appropriate site for misunderstandings, and it articulates also the labyrinthine and tortured logic of Catholic theology, as Ward sees it. It is in the garden, by the bowling-green, that Laura and Helbeck quarrel about his membership of the third order of St Francis. Laura feels it separates them:

> 'As it is, I seem to have nothing to do with half your life – there is a shut door between me and it.' A flash of natural, of wholly irresistible feeling passed through him. He stooped and kissed her hair. 'Open the door and come in!' he said in a whisper that seemed to rise from his inmost soul. (Book IV, Chapter 2)

The garden cannot become the place of erotic union, unless Laura accepts also the patriarchal authority of the Church – the finger relic as patriarchal phallus. Indeed, the voice which here employs the words of the lover in the Song of Songs, calling his beloved into the garden, turns quickly, under the influence of his ecclesiastical advisors, to that of the huntsman:

> There were many moments indeed in which the whole Catholic system appeared to Laura's strained imagination as one vast chasse – an assemblage of hunters and their toils – against which the poor human spirit that was their quarry must somehow protect itself, with every possible wile or violence. (Book IV, Chapter 3)

The chasse, in all its trappings of chivalric order and violence, had indeed proved a potent image for the late nineteenth-century Catholic poets, Gerard Manley Hopkins and Francis Thompson. The latter's 'The Hound of Heaven' (1893) begins:

> I fled him down the nights and down the days . . .
> Up vistaed hopes I sped;
> And shot, precipitated,
> Adown Titanic glooms of chasmed fears,
> From those strong feet that followed, followed after.
> But with unhurrying chase,
> And unperturbèd pace,
> Deliberate speed, majestic instancy
> They beat –[7]

There is the same fear, in Thompson's poem, of being broken up, of being, indeed, 'a broken fount'. To Thompson, as to Laura, the desire to give way, to submit, is strong. But where the poet seeks shelter from the chase, Laura faces it out.

In the manner of Charlotte Brontë's heroines, Laura Fountain provokes her lover,

67

whether in order to challenge his assumption of authority over her, to tease, or to explore the extent of that which divides them. Laura must stand firm against the chasse, not only to preserve her sense of complete and impregnable selfhood, but in order to witness to the faith, or rather unfaith, of her father. In this way, Mary Ward, who punishes terribly any female assertion of independence in her novels, aims to justify and render unthreatening the sight of a woman setting herself up in opposition to male authority. This is a new departure for her, since in all her novels hitherto, there has been a plot involving the foolish assertion of will by a woman character, which is then followed by a somewhat melodramatic chastisement by the man she harms, and finally submission in his arms. Even in *Helbeck*, Laura's defiance of Helbeck's wishes in taking a day trip to the shipworks at Froswick (Workington) to visit Mason, precipitates an horrific accident at the furnace, and Laura's subsequent stranding at Braeside (Grange-over-Sands) in the company of Mason, whom she suspects of improper intentions. The shifting sands of Morecambe Bay become Biblical in the insecurity of their promise of rescue, like the untrustworthy house built on sand in Jesus's parable, and Laura takes to the fells to elude Mason, arriving back at Bannisdale at dawn. At this point of Laura's exhaustion and humiliation, Helbeck's power over her is given all the force of moral and religious backing. Even his garden, of which the narrator so disapproves, is given 'its moment of glory', as it awakes to love like a sleeping beauty:

A huge green lion showed his jaw, his crown, his straight tail quivering in the morning breeze; a peacock nodded stiffly on its pedestal; a great H that had been reared upon its post-supports before Dryden's death stood black against the morning sky, and everywhere between the clumsy crowding forms were roses, straggling and dew-drenched, or wall-flowers in a June wealth of bloom, or peonies that made a crimson flush amid the yews. (Book III, Chapter 3)

This scene, pre-Raphaelite in its detailed and colourful intensity, forms the passionate background to Helbeck's declaration of love for Laura, whom he discovers there, asleep:

She looked up at him as she had never looked before – with a sad and spiritual simplicity as though she had waked in a world where all may tell the truth, and there are no veils left between man and woman . . . One might have fancied her clothed already in the heavenly supersensual body, with the pure heart pulsing visibly through the spirit frame. (Book III, Chapter 3)

The lovers are, for the moment, in a Dante Gabriel Rossetti paradise of lovers' union beyond the grave – the blessed damozel and her suitor reunited – and Ward includes a Rossettiesque touch of surrealism in the exposure of a very physical heart, a secularized version of Christ's own sacred heart, which I have already linked to Helbeck, and which is revealed by his drawing back his robe.

But unlike the 'resurrection' scene in Chapter 37 of *Jane Eyre*, beyond the purgatorial fires of Thornfield, in which a chastened and maimed Rochester accepts the love and help of a newly independent Jane, here all the moral cards are dealt to Helbeck. Where Jane is strong, Laura is a 'little form'; her 'soul and body were too weak'. And yet, somehow this male ascendancy to which Ward normally adheres, must be reversed, so that reason, the nineteenth-century, and Arnoldian values finally prevail. First, although Ward allows Laura to challenge Helbeck, she removes any sense of freewill from her actions. Laura is presented as much as a creation of environment and heredity as Hardy's Tess. Her Cambridge mentor, Dr Friedland, berates her father for failing to educate Laura in the reasons for the beliefs she is brought up to assert. 'It is like an heir – flung to the gypsies. Then you put her to the test – sorely – conspicuously. And she stands fast. But it is a blind instinct, carried through at what a cost!' (Book V, Chapter 1).

And yet, Laura does, independently, find arguments which call Helbeck 'out of his tent', in real challenge. In the Radcliffean Gothic novel, it is common to find the orphaned heroine opposing the will of her tyrannical guardian, and finding the strength so to act in loyalty to family honour, especially loyalty to her father. Since Laura's father is dead, there is as much assertion of her self as of patriarchal adherence in such a move. Laura comes to see her father as someone to be protected, rather than propitiated. And when, having agreed, for a second time, to marry Helbeck, and also now to become a Catholic, Laura realises she has made a mistake, she hears her father's voice – 'Laura, you cannot do it' – but 'it was not his only; it was the voice of my own life, only far stronger and crueller that I had ever known it' (Book V, Chapter 4).

A second way in which Ward ensures the supremacy of the agnostic viewpoint is shown in the way she begins to confuse the discrete symbolic territories she had constructed for her protagonists. Laura comes to be associated, not just with the natural surroundings of Bannisdale, the rock seats and crags of its park, the waters of the River Greet (the Kent) which flows through it, but also with the house itself. From the beginning, Laura had admired Helbeck's Romney (who was born in the county), showing a young bride of the house in her wedding veil:

Its sweet confiding air, – as of one cradled in love, happy for generations in the homage of her kindred and the shelter of the old house, – stood for all the natural human things that creeds and bigots were always trampling under foot. (Chapter 3)

Laura champions the cause of this lady, whose sale to raise money for Catholic orphanages is sometimes threatened, and thereby she asserts another, rival line of family tradition, of domestic piety, and private virtue. For although it retains, as Levens does today, the Spanish leather panelling, the magnificent wooden overmantels, and plaster-work ceilings, the Bannisdale of Helbeck's ultramontane piety has been stripped of its paintings, silver and furniture, all in the cause of philanthropy. It is Laura who grieves for the denuded house, who tends its garden, and claims the first loyalty even of its dogs.

Laura's place within Bannisdale is guaranteed after her return through the park after a Maytime tryst with Mason. A local man sights her hooded figure gliding through the gate into the garden, and believes he has seen 'the grey lady', the ghost of a gypsy once refused admission to the house. This legend is indeed one pertaining to Levens Hall, along with the woman's curse, that no male heir should live to inherit Levens until the Kent had ceased to flow. Laura's natural physical presence in the park has to remain a secret to protect her reputation. But, by means of this event Laura becomes both a tradition of the house, and 'uncanny', which in German is *unheimlich*, or 'not-at-home' – of the house, but not of it. The irony of this is that it is Laura who belongs to the contemporary world, and who is flesh-and-blood, while it is Alan and his house who are lost in a dream of past religious triumphs, and martyrdoms.

In *The Mysteries of Udolpho* (1794), and other Gothic novels, it is the tyrant's captive, the heroine, who proves to be the true heir of his castle, and who finally inherits. Mary

Figure 4.4: Window from the old church, Cartmel Fell.
Photograph by Alison Milbank.

Ward enables Laura to assert her place as, in some sense, heir to Bannisdale, but also heir to the agnosticism of her father, by the manner of her death. Seeing the impossibility of her situation, and shocked by the sudden death of Augustina, her stepmother, who dies before she could be told the good news about her heretic stepdaughter's desire to receive instruction, Laura drowns herself in the River Greet, falling from the otter-cliff, to be carried by the torrent to the same little beach where Helbeck's grandfather's body was washed up. Her end is exquisitely ambiguous in its significance. 'The tyrant river that she loved, had received her, had taken her life', suggests both a return to the natural world from which she sprang, and the element after which she is named, but also a tragic act of identification with the tyrannical power of the Bannisdale estate, to which the river belongs, and its tradition which in some way, Laura had grown to love. For Catholicism too is constantly referred to in terms of an engulfing flood. It beats, for example, through Augustina's 'meagre life, as the whole Atlantic may run pulsing through a drifting reed'. Alan and Laura's love is compared to a river, with Catholic dogma as rocks in its flow. A true follower of her creator's uncle, Matthew Arnold, who stressed the religious role of poetry over that of dogma, Laura Fountain trusts herself to the power of natural symbols to generate a plethora of meanings, and especially to water with its associations with both mutability and new life.

So, is Laura's suicide an act of freedom, or one of submission? It means freedom in terms of preserving her will from the onslaught of sacerdotal tyranny, but it means also a Romantic alliance with the static and tragic aspects of recusant history. Helbeck raises the dead body, only for it to drop gently 'in a last, irrevocable submission'. This submission is both total obedience – to death – and heretical assertion of will in committing suicide, a mortal sin in Catholic moral theology.

Perhaps there is a measure of accommodation between Catholic past and agnostic future in Laura's burial place. She is carried to 'a little chapel high in the hills', which can only be the old church at Cartmel Fell. There, when estranged from Helbeck, Laura had found him in a fragment of medieval glass in the east window, showing a priest holding the host. In the same window of the (Catholic) seven sacraments, she identified a woman waiting for anointing with her stepmother, the Catholic Augustina.(Figure 4.4) This chapel is now a protestant place of worship. Laura's funeral is held inside, but then, unbeliever as she is, her body is carried outside, to a grave overlooking Bannisdale woods. So the history of the little chapel articulates and unites the stages of religious development. The closeness of the sacramental figures gives significance to Laura's fall into what the frontispiece of the novel calls the river Acheron, the river of death. By entering this river Laura finds the baptism and communion, as well as the unction that the Catholic finds in the mass or communion: 'Her [Nature's] rivers were deep and clear for all . . . What need for other sacrament or sign than these?'.

I mentioned Hardy earlier in relation to Mrs Humphry Ward's interest in the effect of environment on character. Her sense of the tragic nature of the retired Westmorland landscape, and its inhabitants is redolent of Hardy's *The Woodlanders* (1887). Hardy's similarly virginal and nymphlike heroine unites nature and culture in her person, and submits, in a mantrap, to her masterful lover. But whereas Grace Melbury is educated out of true empathy with her sylvan environment (just as 'grace' is separated from 'nature' in theological definition), and ends her days, querulously, in provincial drawing-rooms, Laura grows closer, until, like the nymph Daphne, she becomes an actual part of 'the wider and more tragic aspects of this mountain land'.

Notes

1. *A Catalogue of the Caricatures of Max Beerbohm,* compiled by Rupert Hart-Davis (London, 1972), p. 24, no.37. It was first published in *The Poets' Corner* in 1904.
2. William S. Peterson, *Victorian Heretic: Mrs Humphry Ward's Robert Elsmere* (Leicester, 1976), p. 45, quoting an article by a school-friend of Mary Ward, Margaret L. Woods, 'Mrs Humphry Ward: A Sketch from Memory', *Quarterly Review*, ccxxxiv (July, 1920), 148. The new biography by John Sutherland, *Mrs Humphrey Ward: Eminent Victorian, Pre-Eminent Edwardian* (Oxford, 1990), is also interesting on the traumas of Mary Ward's childhood.
3. See *The Howarth Edition of the Life and Works of Charlotte Brontë and her Sisters*, with Introductions to the Works by Mrs Humphry Ward (London, 1902), I, xxi.
4. *Robert Elsmere* is available in the World's Classics series, edited by Rosemary Ashton (Oxford, 1987); *Marcella*, Ward's novel of a young girl's entanglement in radical politics, is published by Virago, with an introduction by Tamie Walters (London, 1984); *Helbeck of Bannisdale*, edited by Brian Worthington, is part of the Penguin English Library (Harmondsworth, 1983).
5. Petersen, p. 97.
6. Mary Ward to Thomas Arnold, 15 November 1896. Pusey House Archive.
7. *The Works of Francis Thompson* (London, 1913), p. 133.

Chapter Five

Ruskin's Views: Gloom and Glory in Kirkby Lonsdale

Keith Hanley

The outlook over the Vale of Lune to which the visitor's gaze is drawn nowadays at Kirkby Lonsdale as 'Ruskin's View' is fraught with ambiguities. What we see, as the given name suggests, has been so influenced by Ruskin's having called our attention to it that it has come to be something much more than a particularly notable beauty spot, and remains what Ruskin made it: a focus of the continuing national debate about the values of natural beauty.

(1)

The View already had a history when Ruskin singled it out for notice in 1875 – one associated particularly with the first of two tours that Turner made through northern England in 1816 of which David Hill has made a detailed study. Turner had made a series of sketches along an itinerary 'from Skipton, through North Lancashire, Gordale, Swaledale, Wensleydale, Teesdale, Westmorland, and Lonsdale back to Skipton'[1] for the projected *General History of the County of York*, by the antiquarian writer, Thomas Dunham Whitaker, and was to have supplied 120 subjects in all, but Whitaker died, and the work was left incomplete. The only pieces Turner was to finish were twenty published in a component of Whitaker's scheme, *The History of Richmondshire* (1823), nine in the *Picturesque Views of England and Wales* series (1827–38), and some other individual pieces.

Turner had a life-long passion for the scenes covered in this tour. His visit to the north provided the vision of a different world from the dinginess of his boyhood in Covent Garden and Wapping described by Ruskin in his chapter in *Modern Painters* volume V (1859), 'The Two Boyhoods', and the scenery he encountered there from his first visit in 1797 represented what was to remain his most affirmative vision of England. As Ruskin wrote, this formative aesthetic experience determined the way he was to see landscapes on future tours around other parts of Europe:

> But Turner evidently felt that the claims upon his regard possessed by those places which first had opened to him the joy, and the labour, of his life, could never be superseded; no Alpine cloud could efface, no Italian sunbeam outshine, the memory of the pleasant dales

Figure 5.1: J. M. W. Turner, *Heysham and Cumberland Mountains*, 1818.
Reproduced with the permission of the Department of Prints and Drawings of the British Museum.

and days of Rokeby and Bolton and many a simple promontory, dim with southern olive,
– many a low cliff that stooped unnoticed over some alien wave, was recorded by him
with a love, and delicate care, that were the shadows of old thoughts and long-lost delights,
whose charm yet hung like morning mist above the chanting waves of Wharfe and Greta.[2]

Ruskin thought the twenty drawings published in *Richmondshire* were a highpoint of
Turner's career, completely free from those darker, tragic undertones of nineteenth-century civilisation that Ruskin was to interpret in Turner's later works when in 1857–8, as
one of his executors, he came to arrange and classify the works that Turner had
bequeathed to the nation. In *The Elements of Drawing* (1857), for example, Ruskin
particularly admired in their composition 'The kind of harmony' he describes in Turner's
'Heysham and Cumberland Mountains' (Figure 5.1):

> the entire purpose of the painter is to give us the impression of wild, yet gentle, country
> life, monotonous as the succession of noiseless waves, patient and enduring as the rocks;
> but peaceful, and full of health and quiet hope, and sanctified by the pure mountain air
> and baptismal dew of heaven, falling softly between days of toil and nights of innocence.
> (15.210)

These drawings evoked an England apparently prior to that of the Industrial Revolution,
and celebrated rural occupations and ways of life that showed no signs of being under
threat by a new age. It was an England of northern rivers and picturesque piles that Ruskin

had himself got to know in his first twelve years, when his parents had arranged summer tours that combined his wine-merchant father's commercial travels with educational visits to places of historic interest and natural beauty. He was able to remember Turner's north as over the years it changed before his eyes. Turner's very itinerary round Morecambe Bay, for example, over the sands at low tide, was different from the one that would have been likeliest after the opening of the Ulverston and Carnforth Railway in 1857.

The overall vision is captured in one of the finest of the completed watercolours, 'Crook of Lune, Looking towards Hornby Castle' (Figure 5.2), seen from the 'station' above the Lancaster main road that had been particularly recommended by a series of connoisseurs of the picturesque. Thomas Gray's journal letter to Thomas Warton, 18 October 1769 (published 1775), on his visit to the Lake District, described

> the river Lune winding in a deep valley, its hanging banks clothed with fine woods, through which you catch long reaches of the water, as the road winds about at a considerable height above it.[3]

Gray's friend and the editor of his letters, William Mason, used the journal letter as a guide and influentially identified 'the view in perfection' that could be obtained three miles from Lancaster, where 'Every feature, which constitutes a perfect landscape of the extensive sort, is here not only boldly marked, but also in its best position.'[4] Thomas West, in his *A Guide to the Lakes . . . in Cumberland, Westmorland and Lancashire*

Figure 5.2: J. M. W. Turner, *Crook of Lune, looking towards Hornby Castle*, 1817–18.
Reproduced with the permission of the Courtauld Institute Galleries.

(1778), and later Wordsworth from the third edition of his *Guide to the Lakes* (1822) reinforced the popularity of this prospect which above all represented the harmony of man and nature. Gray had first written of it as a 'rich and beautiful enclosed country',[5] and William Wilberforce, in his *Journey to the Lake District from Cambridge* (written in 1779), remarked on the effect as that of 'An exceedingly rich cultivated Valley in which Villages & Gentlemen's seats are everywhere visible sufficiently to give the View an air of Population.'[6]

When Whitaker inevitably evokes the same spot in *Richmondshire* the tradition of response to a specifically English landscape beauty has established it as the epitome of the national aesthetic:

> If, setting aside every idea of accommodation, beauty alone had been attended to in the choice of a situation for a capital, of perhaps the finest valley in the kingdom, Kirkby Lonsdale must have been the place. On a plain above the Lune, sufficiently elevated to command the soft foreground, where that river, already majestic and powerful, makes a graceful curve about a peninsula of meadow and pasture, exuberantly fertile, and spotted with standard forest trees, while this soft scene is contrasted by the noblest of backgrounds, the long ridge of Gray Garth, and the towering height of Ingleborough to the south-east, and the piked points of Howgill to the north ... I know not that the site of Kirkby Lonsdale, however admired, has ever been applauded beyond its deserts.[7]

Whitaker added a note of criticism about the parish church of St. Mary the Virgin in the town, regretting the loss 'of all its characteristic features, leaded roof, battlements, pinnacles, and clear story; in place of which has been substituted a long sweeping roof of blue slate, which might better have become the tithe barn of the place.'[8] He did not, however, describe the view from the churchyard which he required Turner to illustrate, and which Hill believes was suggested by Wordsworth's advice to the visitor to 'by no means omit looking at the Vale of Lune from the Churchyard.[9] Here, however, Hill is in error, as the recommendation did not appear, as he supposes, in the original 1810 edition of Wordsworth's *Guide*, but for the first time only in the third edition of 1822. (Figure 5.3) Hill argues interestingly that Turner had difficulty in discovering any distinctive features in the scene, and consequently made a separate trial drawing, labelled 'the continuation of the K. L. C[hurch]yd View', from Casterton Hall to Ingleborough which Hill suggests Turner might have wished Whitaker to adopt instead.[10] So unspecific was the requested view that Turner had to get 'Kirby Lonsdale' (sic) inscribed on a gravestone in the engraving to specify the location.

Certainly, as Hill notes, 'Turner exaggerated the height of the hills and emphasised the meandering rhythms of the river',[11] and the foreground, with the schoolboys' odd game, is unusually diverting. But the impression of the scene beyond is of a more distanced and literally less earthy reprise of the scenery of 'Crook of Lune', framed by the 'woody stiffness ... and inventive grace of the upper boughs' (3.586) in the foreground that in *Modern Painters* volume I (1842) he saw as characteristic of Turner's finest tree-drawing, and reproducing a light-effect that he judged to be that of half an hour after sunrise, with 'Light mists lying in the valleys.' (3.421) Ruskin preferred the churchyard scene to Turner's version of the more famous view, and in the diary entry that he wrote from Bolton Bridge, 24 January 1875, published in Letter LII (1 April 1875) of *Fors Clavigera*, (issued from 1871–84), he writes:

Figure 5.3: J. M. W. Turner, *Kirkby Lonsdale Churchyard*, 1817–18.
Private collection; reproduced with the owner's permission.

The Valley of the Lune at Kirkby is one of the loveliest scenes in England – therefore, in the world. Whatever moorland hill and sweet river, and English forest foliage can be at their best, is gathered there; and chiefly seen from the steep bank which falls to the stream side from the upper part of the town itself. There, a path leads from the churchyard out of which Turner made his drawing of the valley, along the brow of the wooded bank, to open downs beyond; a little bye footpath on the right descended steeply through the woods to a spring among the rocks of the shore. I do not know in all my own country, still less in France or Italy, a place more naturally divine, or a more priceless possession of true 'Holy Land.' (28.298–9)

(2)

Ruskin's letter, from the series addressed to the workmen of England, rejecting modern civilisation and calling for cultural reform, introduces a new level of seriousness. In his reading of Turner's representation, the 'pricelessness' of the scene derived from its association with human sympathies, which in *Modern Painters* volume IV he argues is the 'perfection' of the '*Turnerian Picturesque.*' (6.25–6) '(T)he notable and most pathetic drawing of the Kirkby Lonsdale churchyard' is cited as an example, 'with the schoolboys making a fortress of their larger books on the tombstone, to bombard with the more

76

Figure 5.4: John Ruskin, engraving of J. M. W. Turner's *Egglestone Abbey*, from the Library Edition of *The Works of John Ruskin*, ed. E. T. Cook and Alexander Wedderburn, 1903–12.

projectile volumes'. (6.26) Ruskin's point becomes clearer when he discusses the solemnity of Turner's last great drawings later in the same volume, and refers to the earlier 'introduction of the boys at play in the churchyard of Kirkby Lonsdale' as evidence of a recurrently 'acute sense of the contrast between the careless interest and idle pleasures of daily life, and the state of those whose time for labour, or knowledge, or delight, is passed for ever.' (6.381)

What Ruskin found in the 'Turnerian Picturesque' was above all human meaning – signs of use and value. In one of 'The Three Lectures on Landscape' which he delivered as the Slade Professor of Fine Art at Oxford in January and February 1871, Ruskin offered an exemplary reading of another drawing from Turner's northern tour, 'Egglestone Abbey', which Ruskin himself acquired. (Figure 5.4) Without human traces, he comments, the scene would be 'physically . . . a mere bank of grass above a stream with some wych-elms and willows.' (22.16)

Historical materiality emerges in noticing the *nearly* wild copse wood, 'a cart and rider's track . . . and . . . the scattered ruins of the great abbey' (22.16). Examining in more detail, Ruskin sees that wood and ruin specifically evoke the life of the fourteenth century, and then that the outhouses and refectory have been turned into a farmhouse. An inferential reading then begins to develop: the economic 'innocence' of the absence of fencing, and the cleanliness of rural labour in the eye-catching whiteness of the cow in the mill-pool and of the wood-smoke, and in the washing having been inapprehensively laid out on the stones of the river bed.

At the time of writing the earlier volumes of *Modern Painters* – a work that was, of course, undertaken specifically to interpret and promote the virtues of Turner's landscape art – Ruskin still saw something of the revelation of natural theology in the physical world. In *Modern Painters* volume II (1846), he wrote that

> it is not possible for a Christian man to walk across so much as a rood of the natural earth, with mind unagitated and rightly poised, without receiving strength and hope from some stone, flower, leaf, or sound, nor without a sense of a dew falling upon him out of the sky (4.215–16).

Though he gradually came to see the image of a fallen human nature as inerasable from the contemporary natural environment, and renounced his belief in the literal scheme of Christian redemption, he retained a conviction in the ethical efficacy of natural experience wherever it had been preserved from signs of human corruption:

> but I think, that of the weaknesses, distresses, vanities, schisms, and sins, which often even in the holiest men diminish their usefulness, and mar their happiness, there would be fewer if, in their struggle with nature fallen, they sought for more from nature undestroyed. (4.216)

He sustained a feeling for the sacredness of nature that represented the harmonious relation between the human and the natural in which neither term dominated to produce the inhuman or the unnatural. Mirrored in the softened 'gathering' of 'moorland hill and sweet river, and English forest foliage' he saw the unspoilt promise of a national Christian tradition: a structure of feeling that, confronting the knowledge of mortality in the foreground of the churchyard, displaced the dogmatic consolations of the absent church onto nature itself. It was a position that made nature, if no longer theological, even more crucial as the basis of national education and social wholesomeness. But the only language for expressing the sacred value of nature was still that of the Bible – 'the spring among the rocks', 'the true "Holy Land"' – though it had become more than ever rooted in real locations.

In chapters on 'The Mountain Gloom' and 'The Mountain Glory' in *Modern Painters* volume IV, he examined how the effectiveness of natural education could be wiped out. Why was it that Swiss peasants, living amid scenes of such great beauty, did not enjoy a corresponding cultural elevation? 'For them,' he wrote, 'There is neither hope nor passion of spirit; for them neither advance nor exaltation . . . No books, no thoughts, no attainments, no rest'. (6.388) At that time, he attributed the *gloom* of their life-style to the practices of Roman Catholicism that distorted the immediate influences of nature, and though by the end of that decade he had seen through the flimsiness of this sectarian prejudice it had nevertheless impressed on him the primacy of social and cultural conditioning in determining the break-down of a controlling relation with nature. By *Unto This Last* (1860), he had formed a sure diagnosis of the alienation of modern European civilisation from what he saw as the organic principles of nature-based communities – economic cooperation and social harmony – in the aggressive individualism and materialist acquisitiveness of 'political economy'.

In 'Mountain Glory', however, he states his faith in the edifying power of the relation between man and nature whenever it *is* enabled. While he realised that it would not necessarily operate – 'various institutions have been founded among (the mountains) by the banditti of Calabria as well as by St Bruno' (6.432) – yet he makes the overriding claim, for example, that the cultural achievements of the Greeks and Italians derived from 'their mountain scenery'. (6.426) He suggests an educational experiment to prove his point: 'The matter could only be *tested* by placing for half a century the British universities at Keswick and Beddgelert, and making Grenoble the capital of France' (6.439). It was to further the effects of this relation that Ruskin did so much to promote the teaching of art both at the Working Men's College and Oxford University, including his unsuccessful appeal to the Vice-Chancellor of Oxford in 1884 to purchase 'Crook of Lune' and 'Kirkby Churchyard' for the university's Turner Collection. (37.476).

The idea that an unspoilt natural environment would provide the best context for a system of national education freed from the destructive effects of industrialisation and economic competitiveness was to recur in the debates between traditionalists and entre-preneurs. There was always the danger, however, that the traditions being defended could become far less lively than the dynamism of economic development. Campbell Fraser, Professor of Logic at Edinburgh, for example, who was active in opposition to the extension of railways in the Lake District, was to describe the region as 'nature's own English University in the age of great cities', but he argued lamely that it should 'bar the entrance of the Stygian locomotive'.[12]

(3)

As W. G. Collingwood, Ruskin's sometime secretary and first biographer, notes, 'when Ruskin says that "every prospect pleases," he is going to say – "only man is vile"'.[13] The principal point of Ruskin's notice was to offer the actual churchyard view in 1875 as a representation of desecration: 'more ghastly signs of modern temper than I yet had believed possible'. (28.298) A national *glory* had been turned into a symptom of a national *gloom*:

Well, the population of Kirkby cannot, it appears, in consequence of their recent civilization, any more walk, in summer afternoons, along the brow of this bank, without a fence. I at first fancied this was because they were usually unable to take care of themselves at that period of the day: but saw presently I must be mistaken in that conjecture, because the fence they have put up requires far more sober minds for safe dealing with it than ever the bank did; being of thin, strong, and finely sharpened skewers, on which if a drunken man rolled heavily, he would assuredly be impaled at the armpit. They have carried this lovely decoration down on both sides of the woodpath to the spring, with warning notice on ticket, – 'This path leads only to the Ladies' well – all trespassers will be prosecuted' – and the iron rails leave so narrow footing that I myself scarcely ventured to go down, – the morning being frosty, and path slippery, – lest I should fall on the spikes. The well at the bottom was choked up and defaced, though ironed all round, so as to look like the 'pound' of old days for strayed cattle: they had been felling the trees too; and the old wood had protested against the fence in its own way, with its last root and branch, – for the falling trunks had crashed through the iron grating in all directions, and left it in already rusty and unseemly rags, like the last refuse of a railroad accident, beaten down among the dead leaves. (28.299–300)

The well-springs of Christian civilisation were indeed dried up. 'Ladies', as he footnotes, is a genteel corruption of 'Our Lady's', and the source of what were locally thought to be wonderfully curative powers (especially for sore eyes) was cut off. The 'lovely decoration' of iron railings is made to bear a host of iconographic overdeterminations from 'recent civilization'. As hostile fencing excluding 'trespassers', it evokes the ongoing privatisation of common land by local families, particularly the enclosure of the Kirkby Lonsdale Common effected in 1810 – further recalled in the reference to the pound and the rights of common pasture – that was denying access to the sources of natural education. '[N]o trespassing' he writes a little later in this letter, '(except by lords of the manor on poor men's ground)' (28.302). Such aggressive appropriations of the environment had led to incidents like the famous abatement of the enclosure of Berkhamsted Common on 6 March 1866 when 120 navvies were secretly transported from Euston station by supporters of the Open Space Movement to crow-bar the metal railings and posts away.[14]

On the other hand, the freedoms Ruskin appealed for were embarrassed by a fear of populist and liberalising trends, and he had argued in a magazine essay later published in *Munera Pulveris* (1872) that national *'treasuries . . . should be severely restricted in access and use'* (17.240) if that for which they were valued were not to become destroyed. As Ruskin's radical impulses were controlled by such a committed conservatism, he would surely have shared the rough sense of irony that attached to the nickname for the stepped path, that, while it technically preserved access, actually blighted the view. The local historian, Alexander Pearson, writes that the person responsible for the new 'long and steep flight of steps leading down to the river which [were] known as the "Radical Steps"' was 'a very strong liberal':

In the year 1820, the late Dr.Francis Pearson . . . obtained an order of Quarter Sessions to divert the public footpath to the river, which paths ran through his garden at Abbots Brow; and the steps, which in 1829 consisted of 46 with eleven landings, but are now many more, formed the footpath that was provided to replace them. There was a good deal of opposition at the time and it is supposed that this name was tacked on to them by reason of Dr. Pearson's radical politics.[15]

Ruskin aspired to a Romantic continuity from the local to the cosmic, but its obvious break-down in his own age made him particularly jealous of the inviolability of beautiful retreats, which he felt were likely to be encroached on by an increasingly unsympathetic populace. Peter Fuller has written about such 'holy places', or enclosed gardens, as representing the transformation of the sacred into natural beauty in the course of the last century,[16] and Ruskin retained a belief that they could still provide the basis of local pockets of cultural formation. The years 1874 and 1875, during the terminal mental decline of the young woman whom Ruskin had long wished to marry, Rose la Touche (she died in May, 1875), were perhaps the most sorrowful of his life, but from 1874 to 1886 he addressed a series of letters 'to the sister Ladies of the Thwaite, Coniston' – the Beever sisters – who provided a consolatory friendship that stemmed from their shared daily experience of the 'peace, beauty, and pride of English Shepherd Land.' (37.79) Some days before he wrote the *Fors* letter, on 21 January, Ruskin had written from Kirkby

Lonsdale to Susan Beever about his 'very lovely morning drive and still lovelier evening, and full moonrise here over the Lune.' (37.154) A selection from the letters was published in a volume entitled *Hortus Inclusus* (1887), and they reveal an intimate nurture of the affections, mediating between the unmarried sisters' quiet local activities in the vale and Ruskin's far wider cultural interests and interventions, that gives an idea of the kind of organic civilisation he saw being destroyed.

Indeed, he wished the holy places of natural beauty to form the basis of an alternative national culture. In 'The Lamp of Memory' in *The Seven Lamps of Architecture* (1849), Ruskin had echoed the great Burkean image of the country, in both senses, as a national inheritance:

> God has lent us the earth for our life; it is a great entail. It belongs as much to those who are to come after us, and whose names are already written in the book of creation, as to us; and we have no right by anything that we do or neglect, to involve them in unnecessary penalties, or deprive them of benefits which it was in our power to bequeath. (8.233)[17]

Wordsworth's *Guide*, which had deeply influenced Ruskin in his youth, and which had referred to 'the Lakes in the North of England' as 'a sort of national property, in which every man has a right and interest who has an eye to perceive and a heart to enjoy',[18] was an important link in the development of this idea. Ruskin's thinking directly influenced two of the founders of the National Trust, Octavia Hill and Hardwicke Rawnsley, and in some respects the Guild of St George which he started in 1871 was its utopian forerunner.[19] In his second chapter on 'Ruskin and Wordsworth' in *Ruskin and the English Lakes* (1901), Rawnsley acknowledges his own and the nation's indebtedness to 'the trust' that these two writers had confirmed:

> No one who truly cares for the future of Great Britain, can think of this National Resting-ground robbed of its healing charm, – its power to inspire and invigorate the thought of the present, or illustrate and enforce the thought of the past . . . we are false to the trust that they gave the tender earth of the countryside they loved so truly if we will not listen to their spirit words, and strive a well as we may to keep the land of their inspiration a heritage for the helpful thought, the highest pleasure and the fullest peace of the generations yet to be.[20]

One campaign that Wordsworth, Ruskin, and Rawnsley were all dedicated to was the opposition to the spread of railways into the Lake District. Ruskin footnoted his announcement in the *Fors* letter that he had 'been driving by the old road from Coniston . . . through Kirkby Lonsdale': 'Frightened, (I hear it was guessed in a gossiping newspaper), by the Shipton accident' (28.298). On Christmas Eve, 1874, had occurred the greatest disaster in the history of the Great Western Railway when nine 'coaches tumbled pell mell to destruction over the side of the [Oxford] canal bridge',[21] near Shipton-on-Cherwell, killing 34 passengers and badly injuring 65. It is hardly surprising that the havoc of the felled trees and mangled iron at Kirkby Lonsdale should suggest a kind of disaster that so exactly summarised for him the commercial wreck of the English countryside. It was in this year, 1875, that Robert Somervell organised his protest against the threatened extension of the railway from Windermere to Ambleside and Rydal, and Ruskin contributed the preface to a campaign pamphlet entitled *A Protest against the Extension of Railways in the Lake District* (1876), which consciously emulated

Wordsworth's letters and sonnets to the *Morning Post* in 1841.

As Wordsworth, Ruskin saw that the chief drive behind the proposed railway was commercial profit from dubious mineral deposits decked out in slogans about democratic access. While he was right in drawing attention to the inevitable changes both to the district and the local population that a mass intake of tourism would effect, his attitude to the threat was exaggerated by the radical conflict that he saw behind the issue: could beautiful England become the moral basis of an educational scheme to correct the capitalist machine (he had, after all, spent '[his] own mind, strength, and fortune' on the effort 'to improve the minds of the populace' (34.142), or would that machine devastate beautiful England?

> [A]ll that your railroad company can do for [a working family on holiday] is only to open taverns and skittle grounds round Grasmere, which will soon, then, be nothing but a pool of drainage, with a beach of broken gingerbeer bottles; and their minds will be no more improved by contemplating the scenery of such a lake than of Blackpool. (34.141)

Ruskin's successors were less pessimistic about the problems of access and assets-sharing in the region, but the fight against the railways went on, and in 1883, Rawnsley was active in the appeal against the proposed Honister to Braithwaite line and later contested the Ennerdale Railway Scheme – both of which were withdrawn. But on another major conservation issue led by Somervell that drew Ruskin's sustained fire – the Thirlmere Water Company scheme to provide Mancunians with water – Rawnsley, (who had been a deacon in a working-class suburb of Bristol and knew how much cities needed clean, fresh water), broke ranks. All the same, Manchester Corporation did exploit this need commercially, and drew vast amounts of surplus water to sell on.[22] As Thirlmere was dammed and made into a municipal reservoir, the scenery, that Matthew Arnold had acclaimed in his poem, 'Resignation' (1849), as an unchanging consolation ('Mild hollows, and clear heathy swells, /The cheerful silence of the fells'[23]) for the domestic tragedies that he and his sister, Jane, had endured over ten trying years, was suddenly obliterated. Though Ruskin's absolutism had been compromised, future visitors have had to accept that the submerged scene, however tedious, is at least unpolluting, and even in some sense life-giving.

(4)

Ruskin's paradise garden had suffered a fall – a serpent had entered in. The *Fors* letter continues:

> Just at the dividing of the two paths, the improving mob of Kirkby had got two seats put for themselves – to admire the prospect from, forsooth. And these seats were to be artistic, if Minerva were propitious, – in the style of Kensington. So they are supported on iron legs, representing each, as far as any rational conjecture can extend – the Devil's tail pulled off, with a goose's head stuck on the wrong end of it. Thus:

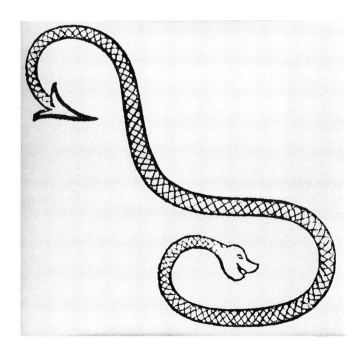

and what is more – two of the geese-heads are without eyes (I stooped down under the seat and rubbed the frost off them to make sure), and the whole symbol is perfect, therefore, – as typical of our English populace, fashionable and other, which seats itself to admire prospects, in the present day. (28.300)

The blind geese-heads, both seated and sat on, had been produced by an insidious kind of surveillance which restricted what was seen. The set prospect itself was to be consumed in a picture-book way that fixed the angle of vision and prevented the spectator from becoming involved in the living landscape. Ruskin's own point of view for the scene is not, in fact, as for Turner's view, a static position in the churchyard, but is rather made up of shifting locations along the path down to the river that provoke his gaze by deflecting it to all the signs of discontinuity between what the scene means for him and the context from which its viewing has been arranged. Brought up on Scott, Ruskin had learned from the novels how a landscape gained depth from the historical details with which it was covered. Scott (as Turner and Ruskin) loved to pore and evoke, and he had written: 'To me the wandering over the field of Bannockburn was the source of more exquisite pleasure than gazing upon the celebrated landscape from the battlements of Stirling Castle'.[24] The kind of art and stage-managing that rebuffed scrutiny was that which impeded a close and faithful observation of nature.

Mason had written of the famously crooked Lune, 'serpentizing'[25] through the meadow, and Turner had exaggerated its coils. But for Ruskin nature was innocent, any seductive temptation derived rather from the decline in human society. In some supplementary manuscript sheets Ruskin notes that from his 'recent studies in *Fors* from Kirkby Lonsdale churchyard' he had drawn the conclusion that 'you cannot . . . at present teach the British public anything but evil, by putting means of information indiscriminately within their reach.'(29.560) The abstraction of artistic forms from their historical contexts was the debasement of aesthetic significance that he associated especially with the Crystal Palace, that had been re-erected in Sydenham between 1851 and 1854 (Figure 5.5), and the South Kensington Museum, established in an iron building in 1857. There was an educational museum in the latter divided into a science section and an art section, which was arranged to illustrate the application of art to industries and to display original works of art in every kind of material:

> You have there casts of the best Greek statues, made entirely accessible to the British public, but at the same time the Soho Bazaar and the Surrey pantomime in the central aisle . . . At Kensington matters are still worse. For there fragments of really true and precious art are buried and polluted amidst a mass of loathsome modern mechanisms, fineries and fatuity (29.560).

At Kensington there was also a gallery of British paintings including some Turners.

Kensington had an additional resonance for Ruskin which surfaces later in the *Fors* letter:

> Considering that Kensington is a school of natural Science as well as Art, it seems to me that these Kirkby representations of the Ophidia are slightly vague. Perhaps, however, in conveying that tenderly sagacious expression into his serpent's head, and burnishing so acutely the brandished sting in his tail, the Kirkby artist has been under the theological

Figure 5.5: The Crystal Palace, from the *Art Journal Catalogue*, 1851.

instructions of the careful Minister who has had his church restored so prettily; – only then the Minister himself must have been, without knowing it, under the directions of another person, who had an intimate interest in the matter. For there is more than failure of natural history in this clumsy hardware. It is indeed a matter of course that it should be clumsy, for the English have always been a dull nation in decorative art; and I find, on looking at things here afresh after long work in Italy, that our most elaborate English sepulchral work, as the Cockayne tombs at Ashbourne and the Dudley tombs at Warwick (not to speak of Queen Elizabeth's in Westminster!) are yet, compared to Italian sculpture of the same date, no less barbarous than these goose heads of Kirkby would appear beside an ass head of Milan. But the tombs of Ashbourne or Warwick are honest, though blundering, efforts to imitate what was really felt to be beautiful; whereas the serpents of Kirkby are ordered and shaped by the 'least erected spirit that fell,' in the very likeness of himself! (28.303)

Alfred Waterhouse was responsible for the design of the Natural History Museum at Kensington (1873–1880), and his abandonment of the neo-classical plans he had been asked to modify together with his taste for Gothic decoration had been heavily influenced by Ruskin's own *Seven Lamps of Architecture*. But Waterhouse could not accept Ruskin's view that 'the use of cast or machine-made ornaments of any kind' was an architectural deceit.[26] His terra cotta decorations, that were intended to be Ruskinian in their profusion, feature animals and plants thematic of a Natural History Museum. Over the main entrance, for example, is a panel representing a lion in the coils of a snake. (Figure 5.6) For Ruskin, this kind of pre-manufactured decoration demonstrated the stifling of art by Mammon, whom in his description of the Fall Milton described as 'the least erected spirit that fell'.[27] It is possible that Ruskin was aware that one of the local great houses, Lunefield, built in 1869–70 for a Bradford manufacturer, Alfred Harris, and situated on the edge of the town about half a mile downstream, had been designed by Waterhouse in the Gothic style he had imbibed from Ruskin with its own private pleasure grounds. Its tower (now demolished) was observable from the churchyard.

The devil-reptile who possesses European cultural and spiritual life in the nineteenth century had gradually become part of one of Ruskin's all-embracing myths since he had been struck by Turner's mythological and apocalyptic oils, exhibited in 1856, particularly *Jason* (1802), *The Goddess of Discord Choosing the Apple of Contention in the Garden of the Hesperides* (1806), and *Apollo and Python* (1811). In 1853 'a series of life-size cement models of extinct species' were constructed 'to inhabit the new Crystal Pal-

Figure 5.6: Terra cotta ornamentation of the British History Museum, from *The Builder*, 1878.

ace gardens at Sydenham',[28] among which was an iguanadon, and in 'The Two Boyhoods' chapter Ruskin notes the resemblance between the guardian dragon in *The Goddess of Discord* and that model 'now guardian of the Hesperidian Gardens of the Crystal Palace' (13.118). Ruskin copied the detail of the dragon which was engraved in *Modern Painters* volume V (Figure 5.7) where he describes it:

> He drags the weight of [his body] forward by his claws, not being able to lift himself from the ground ('Mammon, the least erected spirit that fell') (7.402).

Figure 5.7: John Ruskin, engraving of a detail from J. M. W. Turner's *Garden of the Hesperides*, from *Modern Painters*, volume 5, 1860.

Then he places nineteenth-century England in relation to *its* typifying cult:

> In each city and country of past time, the master-minds had to declare the chief worship which lay at the nation's heart; to define it; adorn it; show the range and authority of it. Thus in Athens, we have the triumph of Pallas; and in Venice the Assumption of the Virgin; here, in England, is our great spiritual fact for ever interpreted to us – the Assumption of the Dragon. (7.408)

Turner himself, as Raymond E. Fitch has written, was Ruskin's 'mythic hero' in the contest he portrayed, 'England's unacknowledged Apollo in combat with the plague of greed in the nineteenth century',[29] just as Ruskin, in the complementary national myth, saw himself as a critical St. George.

In Milton's poem, Mammon takes the lead in the construction of Pandaemonium. Ruskin's letter shows how what the earlier generation of guide book writers had praised as the capital of English beauty could become the capital of hell. The image of the seat-legs turns into an ouroboros, the snake with its tail in its mouth, a symbol for the infernal circularity of the process of manufacturing ugliness:

> For observe the method and circumstance of their manufacture. You dig a pit for ironstone, and heap a mass of refuse on fruitful land; you blacken your God-given sky, and consume your God-given fuel, to melt the iron; you bind your labourer to the Egyptian toil of its castings and forgings; then, to refine his mind you send him to study Raphael at Kensington; and with all this cost, filth, time, and misery, you at last produce – the devil's tail for your sustenance, instead of an honest three-legged stool. (28.303–4)

In 'The Nature of the Gothic' in *The Stones of Venice* volume II (1853), Ruskin explained how the Assyrian and the Egyptian kind of workmanship was enslaving. Inferior workmen were made to lower their method of figure sculpture 'to a standard which every workman could reach, and then trained . . . by discipline so rigid, that there was no chance of [their] falling beneath the standard appointed.' (10.189) He was certain about what this kind of poor execution, from which both aesthetic pleasure and creative fulfilment were excluded, amounted to:

> You do all this that men may live – think you? Alas – no; the real motive of it all is that the fashionable manufacturer may live in a palace, getting his fifty per cent. commission on the work which he has taken out of the hands of the old village carpenter, who would have cut two stumps of oak in two minutes out of the copse, which would have carried your bench and you triumphantly, – to the end of both your times. (28.304)

On the other hand, he saluted a new school of English art, the Pre-Raphaelite Brotherhood, in two influential letters to *The Times* (1851), because its artists

> as far as in them lies, . . . will draw either what they see, or what they suppose might have been the actual facts of the scene they desire to represent, irrespective of any conventional rules of picture-making; and they have chosen their unfortunate though not inaccurate name because all artists did this before Raphael's time, and after Raphael's time did not this, but sought to paint fair pictures, rather than present stern facts (12.322).

Ruskin saw the underside of unlovely habits of living through the facade of village idyllicism:

> Now, not a hundred paces from these seats there is a fine old church, with Norman door, and lancet east windows, and so on; and this, of course, has been duly patched, botched, plastered, and primmed up; and is kept as tidy as a new pin. For your English clergyman keeps his own stage properties, nowadays, as carefully as a poor actress her silk stockings. Well, all that, of course, is very fine; but, actually, the people go through the churchyard to the path on the hill-brow, making the new iron railing an excuse to pitch their dust-heaps, and whatever of worse they have to get rid of, crockery and the rest, – down *over the fence* among the primroses and violets to the river, – and the whole blessed shore underneath, rough sandstone rock throwing the deep water off into eddies among the shingle, is one waste of filth, town-drainage, broken sauce-pans, tannin, and mill-refuse. (28.300–1)

Continuing his journey through the Dales, he found the same glaring discrepancy at Clapham:

> I went down to the brook-side to see the bridge; and found myself instantly, of course, stopped by a dung-hill, – and that of the vilest human sort; while, just on the other side of the road, – not twenty yards off, – were the new schools, with their orthodox Gothic belfry – all spick and span – and the children playing fashionably at hoop, round them, in a narrow paved yard – like debtor children in the Fleet, in imitation of the manners and customs of the West End. High over all the Squire's house, resplendent on the hill-side, within sound alike of belfry, and brook. (28.301)

At Clapham, the squire's house presided over a social sham, with its educational investment summed up by the school's fashionable architectural topping of an 'orthodox Gothic Tower', (which must again have seemed a painful irony to Ruskin), and the institutionally imprisoned children, taken from Dickens's description of the Marshalsea in Chapter VI of *Little Dorrit* (1855–7).

Ruskin was, of course, no more opposed to the Church and feudal order than he was against education. In a subsequent letter in *Fors*, LVI, 1 August 1875, he complains of an article 'from a local paper, urging what it can in defence of the arrangements noticed by me as offensive at Kirkby Lonsdale and Clapham' (28.383), and quotes: ' "The squire's house does not escape, though one can see no reason for the remark unless it be that Mr Ruskin dislikes lords, squires, and clergymen." ' (28.383) As regards the institutions in themselves, he points out that he had always been peculiarly susceptible to the claims of religious tradition and the nobility, humorously recalling how the previous summer he had given alms and a kiss on the lips to a Capuchin friar in Rome, and how accompanying his father on his business trips in childhood, the family had taken every opportunity of visiting the local stately homes, abbeys and castles. It was precisely because of the powerful influence of their cultural patronage that he criticises so bitterly their complicity in what he sees as the decline of civilisation:

> in that glorious England of the future . . . there will be no abbeys (all having been shaken down, as my own sweet Furness is fast being, by the luggage trains); no castles, except such as may have been spared to be turned into gaols, like that of 'time-honoured Lancaster,' also in my own neighbourhood; no parks, because Lord Derby's patent steam agriculture will have cut down all the trees; no lords, nor dukes, because modern civilization won't be Lorded over, nor Led anywhere; no gentlemen's seats, except in Kirkby Lonsdale style; and no roads anywhere, except trams and rails. (28.392–3)

Ruskin had a point in complaining that since 1846 the Furness Railway Company had begun to transport tourists on excursions within yards of the monastic remains. Lancaster Castle, however, had ceased to be a baronial residence and become a prison at least as early as the reign of Henry VIII, though it had become an enlarged and improved institution following the 1788 Act of Parliament. He is certainly unfair to that great Lancashire liberal, Edward Henry Stanley, Earl of Derby, among whose many reforming causes was the acquisition of people's parks. Ruskin had possibly heard tell of Lord Bective's notorious steam-engine causing havoc on the streets of Kirkby Lonsdale.[30]

When he arrived at the next stage on his tour through the Dales, Bolton Bridge and the Abbey, 'to look again at Turner's subject of the Wharfe shore', (he had at one time owned Turner's painting of *Bolton Abbey, Yorkshire* [c.1825]), Ruskin comments:

> If there is one spot in England, where human creatures pass or live, which one would expect to find, in *spite* of their foul existence, still clean – it is Bolton Park. But to my final and utter amazement, I had not taken two steps by the waterside at the loveliest bend of the river below the stepping-stones, before I found myself again among broken crockery, cinders, cockle-shells, and tinkers' refuse; – a large old gridiron forming the principal point of effect and interest among the pebbles. The filth must be regularly carried past the Abbey, and across the Park, to the place. (28.301)

In *Modern Painters* volume V, Ruskin had described the effect on the youthful Turner of this scene, of which in *Modern Painters* volume IV he wrote that 'for all the latter part of his life, [Turner] never could even speak . . . but his voice faltered' (6.303):

> and one summer evening . . . he finds himself sitting alone among the Yorkshire hills. For the first time, the silence of Nature round him, her freedom sealed to him, her glory opened to him. Peace at last; no roll of cart-wheel, nor mutter of sullen voices in the back shop; but curlew-cry in space of heaven, and welling of bell-toned steamlet by its shadowy rock.

Freedom at last. Dead wall, dark railing, fenced field, gated garden, all passed away like the dream of a prisoner; and behold, far as foot or eye can race or range, the moor, and cloud. Loveliness at last. It is here then, among these deserted vales! Not among men. Those pale, poverty-struck, or cruel faces; – that multitudinous, marred humanity – are not the only things that God has made. Here is something He has made which no one has marred. Pride of purple rocks, and river pools of blue, and tender wilderness of glittering trees, and misty lights of evening on immeasurable hills. Beauty, and freedom, and peace (7.383–4).

Wordsworth's *The White Doe of Rylstone* (1815) is set here – a poem inspired by Whitaker's *History and Antiquities of the Deanery of Craven* (1805). It celebrates in the figure of the doe the healing quietism of nature, surviving and calming the grief of religious bloodshed in the Rising of the North of 1569:

There doth the gentle Creature lie
With those adversities unmoved;
Calm spectacle, by earth and sky
In their benignity approved!
And aye, methinks, this hoary Pile,
Subdued by outrage and decay,
Looks down upon her with a smile,
A gracious smile that seems to say-
'Thou, thou art not a Child of Time,
But Daughter of the Eternal Prime!'[31]

Ruskin comments that

doubtless, in Bolton priory, amiable school teachers tell their little Agneses the story of the white doe; – and duly make them sing in psalm tune, 'As the hart panteth after the waterbrooks.'
Very certainly, nevertheless, the young ladies of Luneside and Wharfedale don't pant in the least after their water-brooks; and this is the saddest part of the business to me. Pollution of rivers! – yes, that is to be considered also; – but pollution of young ladies' minds to the point of never caring to scramble by a riverside, so long as they can have their church-curate and his altar-cloths to their fancy, – *this* is the horrible thing, in my own wild way of thinking. (28.301–2)

He did not simply see it as a matter of clearing the rubbish away. The Commission on Water Pollution was in fact sitting at this very time in Kirkby Lonsdale.[32] The problem for him was that its being left there in the first place symptomised the malaise of a culture that had lost contact with the kind of living response to nature that had produced the works of the greatest English Romantic nature poet and painter. Young contemporaries might mouth verses and pedantically observe religious and social practices without any sense of what they had really stood for, or of how they clashed with the material reality of their own historical experience.

Ruskin's shattered idealism was driven by personal suffering and frustration. At times, when it seemed to him that he had lost each one of the persons and things that he had loved, it touches on paranoia. But his fierceness of penetration and his ultra-sensitivity made him *see* more than any other Victorian not only that something was happening very quickly about which too little was being questioned, but also that most English people were becoming incapable of distancing themselves from that process of habituation enough to recognise what he called 'the mystery and shame' of 'the English death – the European death of the nineteenth century'. (7.386–7)

In 1884, Ruskin delivered two lectures at the London Institution entitled 'The Storm-Cloud of the Nineteenth Century' in which he reported on meterological effects he had been noticing since 1871. The main phenomena were a 'plague-wind', causing a continuous trembling of leaves, and the darkening of the sky by spreading and opaque white cloud. He quotes from a diary entry from Bolton Abbey, 4 July 1875, when he began to realise that this wind had a history. It was written some six months after he wrote the *Fors* letter on Kirkby Lonsdale, and in September of the same year he had written from Brantwood to his American friend, Charles Eliot Norton, 'The thing that chiefly tires me ... is the continually dark sky, like a plague'.[33]

Following his experiences in the Dales, Ruskin was beginning to confront his ultimate terror of the death of nature – his fear that the devil-dragon of modern industrial civilisation was physically blotting out the sun, as the source of beauty and life: 'Blanched Sun, – blighted grass – blinded man.' (34.40) In Lecture I of 'The Storm-Cloud', he quotes from a diary entry from Brantwood made in August 1879 in which he describes the 'Manchester devil's darkness' of 'The most terrific and horrible thunderstorm':

> It waked me at six, or a little before – then rolling incessantly, like railway luggage trains, quite ghastly in its mockery of them – the air one loathsome mass of sultry and foul fog, like smoke; scarcely raining at all, but increasing to heavier rollings, with flashes quivering vaguely through all the air, and at last terrific double streams of reddish-violent fire, not forked or zigzag, but rippled rivulets – two at the same instant some twenty to thirty degrees apart, and lasting on the eye at least half a second, with grand artillery-peals following; not rattling crashes, or irregular cracklings, but delivered volleys. (34.37)

Physical and moral are linked verbally in 'the sulphurous chimney-pot vomit of *black-guardly* cloud' (34.38; my italics), and the whole passage is a nightmare orchestration of the key material images of the contemporary economy that are all incorporated in the inchoate overall symbol of Ruskin's belching dragon – the railway rolling-stock, the dirt and heat of industrial processes, and the war machine that at the time of writing was perpetrating British commercial interest in the Second Afghan and Zulu Wars. Ruskin had assuredly depicted the climate of the times.

Ruskin is one of the great English controversialists. Like Swift or Orwell, his critique of what he found most repulsive became distortive and apocalyptic. But his faith in the relation between the human community and its physical environment as the standard of moral health and beauty seems on ever firmer ground. His critical appeal is finally to our instinctive aversion to foulness of all kinds. A. E. Housman recorded a striking lecturing technique of Ruskin's in a letter he wrote as an Oxford undergraduate in 1877:

Figure 5.8: John Ruskin, *Seascale Sands*, 1889.
Reproduced with the permission of The Ruskin Galleries, Bembridge School.

He had got a picture of Turner's, framed and glassed, representing Leicester and the Abbey in the distance at sunset, over a river. He read the account of Wolsey's death out of *Henry VIII*. Then he pointed to the picture as representing Leicester when Turner had drawn it. Then he said, 'You, if you like, may go to Leicester to see what it is like now. I never shall. But I can make a pretty good guess.' Then he caught up a paintbrush. 'These stepping-stones of course have been done away with, and are replaced by a be-au-ti-ful iron bridge.' Then he dashed in the iron bridge on the glass of the picture. 'The colour of the stream is supplied on one side by the indigo factory.' Forthwith one side of the stream became indigo. 'On the other side by the soap factory.' Soap dashed in. 'They mix in the middle – like curds,' he said, working them together with a sort of malicious deliberation. 'This field, over which you see the sun setting behind the abbey, is now occupied in a *proper* manner.' Then there went a flame of scarlet across the picture, which developed itself into windows and roofs and red brick, and rushed up into a chimney. 'The atmosphere is supplied – thus!' A puff and a cloud of smoke all over Turner's sky: and then the brush thrown down, and Ruskin confronting modern civilization amidst a tempest of applause.[34]

Ruskin was at this time playing to a receptive audience at Oxford, but he had been fearlessly denunciatory in his lectures to the manufacturers of Manchester and Bradford on their own territory.

His vision of England is now more than ever not to be balked. The last piece of writing Ruskin ever completed was the closing part of his autobiography, *Praeterita* (1885–9), written at Seascale on the Cumberland coast in 1889. Rawnsley describes the village at that time,

> with its dwarf roses and its purple geraniums full in flower on the sand-hills; and its peep of those hills in the Wastwater direction, as blue as ever the hills were blue which his old nurse sang of, as they crossed the bridge of Tweed.[35]

As he tried to gather the fragments of his life, Ruskin took trips into the surrounding district, to Muncaster Castle and Calder Abbey, and must often have looked out from the dunes, of which he had made two drawings in 1881 and at least one watercolour (1889) (Figure 5.8), one of his last recorded paintings. It shows the beach less than two miles south of Windscale. What he would nowadays have to dash over the glass on this painting has only too fully materialised the foreboding of 'Kirkby Lonsdale style': Sellafield Nuclear Power Station and the boring towers of Nirex U.K. There, parties of schoolchildren are bussed daily for 'educational tours' around Sellafield Business Centre, which advertises itself under the provocative slogan: 'There's more to West Cumbria than just beautiful scenery'.

Notes

1. David Hill, *In Turner's Footsteps: through the hills and dales of Northern England* (London, 1984), p. 27.
2. *Modern Painters* volume IV (1856), Library Edition, *The Works of John Ruskin.* ed. E. T. Cook and Alexander Wedderburn, 39 vols. (London, 1903–12), 6, 303. Further references to this edition are by volume number in the text.
3. *The Works of Thomas Gray*, 2 vols. (London, 1825), II, 343.
4. *Ibid.*
5. *Ibid.*
6. Edited by C. E. Wrangham (Stocksfield, 1983), p. 44.
7. *An History of Richmondshire*, 2 vols. (London and Leeds, 1823), II, 277.
8. *Ibid.*
9. *Wordsworth's Guide to the Lakes*, ed. Ernest de Selincourt (Oxford, 1977), p. 3.
10. See Hill, p. 94.
11. *Ibid.*
12. See Graham Murphy, *Founders of the National Trust* (London, 1987), p. 83.
13. *The Lake Counties* (London, 1902), p. 23 n.1.
14. See Murphy, *op. cit.*, p. 15.
15. *Annals of Kirkby Lonsdale and Lunesdale in Bygone Days* (Kendal, 1930), p. 82.
16. See Peter Fuller, *Theoria: Art and the Absence of Grace* (London, 1988), p. 15.
17. See Edmund Burke, *Reflections on the Revolution in France*, edited by Conor Cruise O'Brien (Harmondsworth, 1988), pp. 119–20.
18. *Guide*, p. 93.
19. The Trust's first property, *Dinas Oleu*, part of the cliff overlooking Cardigan Bay near Barmouth, was given by the Guild's first benefactress, Fanny Talbot.
20. *Ruskin and the English Lakes* (Glasgow, 1901), pp. 187–8.
21. L. T. C. Rolt, *Red for Danger: a History of Railway Accidents and Railway Safety Precautions* (London, 1955), p. 64.
22. See John James Harwood, *History and Description of the Thirlmere Water Scheme* (Manchester, 1895), p. 100ff.
23. *Matthew Arnold*, The Oxford Authors, edited by Miriam Allot and Robert H. Super (Oxford and New York, 1986), p. 42, 11.66–7.
24. Recorded by Lockhart, quoted by James Reed, *Sir Walter Scott: Landscape and*

Locality (London, 1980), p. 10.

25. Gray's *Works*, II, 343,n. Hogarth in *Analysis of Beauty* (1752) and also Mengs and Winckelman saw the 'line of beauty' as serpentine, based on the principle of undulation.

26. Quoted in William T. Stearn, *The Natural History Museum at South Kensington: A History of the British Museum (Natural History) 1753–1980* (London, 1981), p. 44.

27. *Paradise Lost, The Poems of John Milton*, edited by John Carey and Alastair Fowler (London and Harlow, 1968), I, 500, 1.679.

28. Lynn Barber, *The Heyday of Natural History, 1820–1870* (London, 1980), p. 177.

29. *The Poison Sky. Myth and Apocalypse in Ruskin* (Athens, Ohio and London, 1982), p. 393.

30. I am grateful to Mr George Harrison of Kirkby Lonsdale who drew my attention to the local dispute over this vehicle. The relevant documentation is to be found among the draft minutes for the Inspector of Nuisances (1872) in the Records of the Kirkby Lonsdale Local Board at the Cumbria Record Office, Kendal: WPC7–60.

31. *The Poetical Works of William Wordsworth*, edited by Ernest de Selincourt, revised by Helen Darbishire, 5 vols. (Oxford, 1952–9), III, p. 340, 11.1901–10.

32. See 'The Water Supply of Kirkby Lonsdale', *Lancaster Gazette*, 29 May 1875, p. 8.

33. Letter 278, *The Correspondence of John Ruskin and Charles Eliot Norton*, edited by John Lewis Bradley and Ian Ousby (Cambridge, 1987), p. 364.

34. Quoted in full in *The Norton Anthology of English Literature*, 5th edition, vol.2, edited by M. H. Abrams (New York, 1986), p. 1328.

35. *Ruskin and the English Lakes*, pp. 56–7.

Chapter Six

'Arts and Kindliness': Gordon Bottomley and his Circle

Helen Phillips

In the spring of 1904 Edward Thomas and Arthur Ransome both visited Cartmel, to stay with Gordon Bottomley at Well Knowe House.[1] The poet and playwright Gordon Bottomley is now little read. The quality of his work varies enormously: some of it, particularly among the early poems, is quite bizarrely bad, but much of it is by any standards extraordinarily good – in particular, much of the later poetry and the many plays he wrote on Scottish themes in a style based on Japanese *Noh* drama. When Edward Thomas and Arthur Ransome visited Cartmel, it was Bottomley who of the three of them probably seemed the most securely settled into the career of literature, and the most likely to become an established writer. Thomas at twenty-six, having published three books of essays and an edition of Dyer's poems, was making a precarious living from reviewing and commissions. He had a young family to keep and had been ill with depression and overwork most of the preceding year. Ransome, twenty, had just abandoned a university course and set himself up in a room in Chelsea furnished mostly with packing cases, to begin the life of a literary Bohemian, earning a pound a week as errand boy for the nearly defunct Unicorn Press. It was to be another ten years before Thomas started to write the poetry on which his reputation now rests, and 1929 before Ransome wrote *Swallows and Amazons*.

In contrast, Bottomley could write what he wanted, when he wanted: he had money and leisure. It was leisure purchased at a cost. Born in 1874, the son of a Keighley accountant, he suffered from his teens to middle age from tubercular illness, with frequent and prostrating haemorrhages. Yet this had rescued him at eighteen from a career in a Bradford bank. From then on he was free, as free as his illness allowed, to pursue his desire to be a poet and playwright. In 1892 his parents and an aunt – they were a genial, close-knit family – moved with him to Well Knowe House outside Cartmel in the hope that the clean, mild air of North Lancashire would help him. He was often confined to bed, or a sofa outside the house: 'The most immediate medium of art, Words, was the only one open to me – and sometimes I could not afford even the mouthful of air which is their condition of existence'.[2]

To a young man whose boyhood dreams had been to study painting or medicine, whose idols were Oscar Wilde, Arthur Symons, Rossetti, and Symbolist painters like Gustave Moreau and Charles Ricketts – decidedly unrustic tastes – this healthy but remote countryside could have seemed exile and his illness might have bred despair. Instead he had dedicated his life to art: writing, playing early keyboard music, and embarking on what was to become an impressive collection of paintings, drawings and prints (he and his wife bequeathed six hundred items to Carlisle Art Gallery). He kept abreast of what was happening in London and Paris. The turn of the century was an intoxicating time for anyone interested in developments in modern European art and, aesthetically, all his life Bottomley remained a *fin de siecle* man, but he was also a Northerner (born in Yorkshire with Scottish ancestry), and he evolved a philosophy of art that married the two influences. Eventually, in his Scottish *Noh* plays, this union produced writing of considerable originality. (Figure 6.1)

He is most remembered now as the friend of other, greater, artists: Edward Thomas, Arthur Ransome, Isaac Rosenberg, Paul Nash and Charles Ricketts, and I shall begin by looking at his life and friendships before considering his own work. He was an affectionate man, expansive and slightly elaborate in speech, enthusiastic and hospitable. He was also calm and shrewd, and a perceptive critic, with a gift for recognizing talent at a young and struggling stage and offering encouragement, friendship and practical help. He did this for Ransome and Thomas, and later for Nash and Rosenberg.

Figure 6.1: William Rothenstein, Portrait of Gordon Bottomley, 1922.

Reproduced with the permission of Tullie House, Carlyle Art Gallery and Museum.

(1) Edward Thomas, Arthur Ransome and Georgian Poets

He first met both Thomas and Ransome in London. Remissions of his illness allowed him to spend periods in London in 1903, 1904 and 1905. He met Yeats, Binyon, Masefield, and three artists who became lifelong friends: James Guthrie the printer and book-designer, Charles Ricketts and Charles Shannon; and he saw Gordon Craig's revolutionary stage-designs. Bottomley specialised in long-distance friendships, through correspondence, fortified with occasional forays to London and whenever possible by visits to Cartmel by the friends. In 1905 he married Emily Burton from Arnside, a lively woman who shared his interests and friends. It was a very happy marriage.

Bottomley's correspondence with Edward Thomas, begun in 1902, continued unbroken until Thomas's death in 1917. Thomas's most recent biographer[3] considers that of all the artists he knew Bottomley and Guthrie were his most intimate friends: Thomas trusted Bottomley as advisor and confidant in emotional as well as literary matters. Thomas's correspondence with Bottomley is a record of his life and work as a writer as well as of his often tortured psychological states. At the time of his first visit to Cartmel in 1904 his depression was putting great strain on his marriage. Bottomley, now and in the years to come, was a friend who could provide comfort. 'I should not have been so glad to be home so calmly glad, if I had not been glad to be away with you all at Well Knowe . . . ', he wrote after the visit, 'For yourself, you do not need my words on paper. Our happy intimacy needs no compliment, & I dare to think that perhaps you have some recollections – I have many – that make thanks unnecessary. Well Knowe is going into my memory, along with Oxford and the Pilgrim's Road and the Surrey & Wales & Wiltshire I knew as a child'.[4] Since place and memory, and the personal meanings of places, are central to his art this is an important statement. The sources of Thomas's almost continual sense of personal crisis and failure were literary (uncertainty about how he should write) as well as psychological. He found in Bottomley a friend with whom he could be frank about both, and whose advice on both he valued.

For both of them the boyish, ebullient Ransome, was an attractive companion, and an alleviator of Thomas's depression. For a month in the autumn of 1904 Thomas even moved into a room at Ransome's lodgings in London.[5]

In 1904 Bottomley and William Holmes, the skilful Ulverston printer who was publishing Bottomley's *Gate of Smaragdus*, were planning to launch the Lanthorn Press, and arranged that Thomas's *Rose Acre Papers* and Ransome's *The Souls of the Streets* should be the first in a projected series of essays and poetry by young writers.[6] Ransome's autobiography gives an amusing account of Mr Holmes' indulgent dealing with young authors,[7] and slightly fictionalised portraits of both Edward Thomas and Bottomley appear in Ransome's *The Souls of the Streets* (1904) and *Bohemia in London* (1907). Bottomley at the time of his first visit to London appears in the guise of a bankclerk who writes poetry at night, encountered in a Soho coffee house:

A huge felt hat banged freely down over a wealth of thick black hair, bright blue eyes, an enormous black beard, a magnificent manner . . . a way of throwing his head back when he drank, of thrusting it forward when he spoke, an air of complete abandonment to the moment and the moment's thought; he took me tremendously. He seemed to be delighting his friends with impromptu poetry. I . . . carried my pot of beer to his table just beside him, where I could see him better, and also hear his conversation.[8]

The bankclerk-poet pours out a stream of entrancing but – to Ransome – nonsensical talk about Art: 'twaddle, but such downright, spirited, splendid twaddle, flung out from the heart of him in such a grand, careless way that made me think of largesse royally scattered on the mob'.[8] Thomas, too, was all too recognisable in the *Souls of the Streets* as Merlin, a writer whose destructive criticism hurts himself and others:'His sentences are like wasps, beautiful in their first flash of colour, but with an unpleasant sting in their tails . . . He sees so clearly the pettiness of others he cannot believe in the greatness of himself'.[10]

It is not surprising that Ransome, with his robust, no-nonsense stance towards all romanticisms (including his own), should have found Bottomley's *fin de siècle* convictions somewhat absurd. They undoubtedly were somewhat absurd. Bottomley, for his part, was out of sympathy with the tweedy, hearty, ethos of out-of-doors manliness that Ransome and Thomas often espoused: an ethos that became the hallmark of the 'Georgian' literary movement. (It had come into being partly in reaction to the Oscar Wilde trial, and Bottomley, to his credit, never wavered in his admiration for Wilde.)

Despite his amusement, Ransome was drawn to Bottomley and Cartmel, returning to spend the summers of 1905, 1906 and 1907 there, in accommodation found for him by Bottomley with the Towers family at Wall Nook Farm, a few minutes from Well Knowe. The Lake District had long been a magical place for Ransome. Staying at Cartmel gave him the opportunity to visit his beloved Collingwood family at Coniston while remaining independent. At Wall Nook he wrote all morning, then went for long walks or visited Well Knowe, where Bottomley talked or played music. Looking back years later, Ransome wrote:

> At Well Knowe . . . Gordon Bottomley, mild of eye, slow of speech, archiepiscopal in manner, lived with his father, his mother and his aunt . . . As he grew older he outlived the affectations of his youth, wrote many good plays and some lovely poems, such as 'Cartmel Bells', the simplicity of which was in complete contrast to the orchid-house atmosphere of his early verse.[11]

During Ransome's summers at Cartmel and Low Yewdale, the poet Lascelles Abercrombie and Dixon Scott, a young critic, also stayed in the Cartmel neighbourhood. The 'Georgian' era was dawning, when poets turned to country life, labourers, gipsies and tramps for inspiration and celebrated a rural English continuity in landscape, folksong and open-air life. Bottomley believed that the place of nature in art was what he found in Blake, Palmer and Calvert: the visual world reshaped by imaginative or mystical vision. He remained true to the principles of Wilde's *Intentions* or Arthur Symons's *Symbolist Movement*, and his young friends mocked him: Dixon Scott invented the slogan 'Roast beef and Rose-buds' to sum up their own creed.[12] The clothes of this little group reflected their affiliations to contemporary aesthetic schools: Bottomley in his artist's cloak and 'wideawake' hat (fashions of the nineties that he and Emily still favoured in the 1940s); Ransome, Thomas and Abercrombie in countrymen's tweeds. Thomas and Ransome went for long tramps; Thomas went for long swims in the lake; they drank strong local beer, and smoked strong local 'Kendal Twist' tobacco in pipes sweetened by the Coniston charcoal-burners (Edward Thomas liked the short, old-fashioned Cartmel pipes).

Where Ransome was flippant, Thomas from the beginning saw in Bottomley and his writing from the beginning something deeper. Of his earliest play, *The Crier by Night*, a savage melodrama set on the shores of Windermere in the Dark Ages, he said 'It seemed to me to have a perfect unity. . . You hover continually on the verge of what is probably inexpressible. Your success is all the more brilliant'.[13] Bottomley's blank verse, he wrote in a review, was 'perhaps the most delicate of our time'.[14]

Even before they met, Thomas commented in a letter on the rapport he felt with Bottomley. The Bottomleys visited the Thomases at Bearstead and Ashford, and the two writers met sometimes in London. Thomas stayed again in Cartmel in 1906, and in 1907: a wet fortnight,'to walk with me and talk with Gordon Bottomley', as Ransome put it.[15] He walked the southern Lake District fells with Emily and Ransome (Bottomley was amused that Thomas vehemently refused to look at Wordsworth's grave). He liked the 'shrewd and racy' style of local speech, unlike the 'suspicious silence' of southern countryfolk.[16] In the evenings they sat by the fire at Well Knowe, talking, smoking and singing. There was always music at Well Knowe: piano or clavichord, folksongs or Scarlatti. The Bottomleys and their friend George Rathbone were, like Thomas, folksong enthusiasts. Gordon contributed local songs, as well as some of his own poems and prose to books edited by Thomas: 'Poor Old Horse' and the 'Holme Bank Hunting Song', about a fox-chase all over Furness, for example, appear in *The Heart of England* (1907), and after his first visit Thomas complained that 'Cartmel & the larches' kept getting into the book he was writing, *Beautiful Wales* (1905), which includes Bottomley's 'Apple Bluth'.[17] He wrote 'What is the use of writing to you . . . when I have wished for hardly anything in some of the calm evenings here except you and a spinet and "Somer is icomen in"?'[18]

Bottomley, whose father's family were Swedenborgians, rejected conventional Christian belief, and his writings show his readiness to enter wild and morbid states. Thomas could express to him feelings, however negative or neurotic, without fear of boring or shocking:

I have had terrible moods here & long fits of despair & exhaustion . . . I feel as if I would never try to write again. There is no form that suits me, & I doubt if I can make a new form.
I am plagued by . . . whether anything is worth while, whether I shall ever again have hope or joy or enthusiasm or love . . . Shall I ever have the relief of true and thorough insanity?'[19]

Bottomley called him Edward the Confessor; Thomas ended one letter, 'O Comforter, goodbye . . .' Bottomley offered advice: he proposed alternative genres (unsuccessfully), counselled less introspection (unsuccessfully), dissuaded Thomas from opium (successfully), gave criticism and suggestions (often followed), and for many years proof-read for Thomas. The story of how in 1914, through his friendship with Robert Frost, Edward Thomas suddenly, almost magically, found the ability to write poetry, and with it a new contentment of spirit, is well known. The unique importance of Frost in Thomas's self-discovery as a poet can, however, be overstated, as it is in Helen Thomas's moving but mythologizing account of her husband's life[20] and the less spectacular and direct, but nevertheless significant contribution, of the years of discussion and correspondence with Bottomley (and even, in certain respects, of Thomas's admiration for aspects of Bottomley's own poetry) has not received its due.

Between 1907 and 1915 Bottomley was frequently very ill, but the poems in *Chambers of Imagery I* and *II* (1907 and 1912) show new strength and clarity, and the plays after *King Lear's Wife* (completed 1913) use an increasingly free verse. His work, including the delicate and disturbing 'End of the World', appeared in the *Georgian Poetry* anthologies between 1911 and 1919. The macabre elements in his work, born of *fin de siècle* Decadence, brought him around 1911 into alignment with the Georgian poets' exploration of brutal realism, which for a time seemed to many readers the hallmark of modern poetry. *King Lear's Wife*, like Masefield's *Everlasting Mercy*, was seen as epitomizing this trend. *Mrs Lear* (as Bottomley called it) had pride of place in *Georgian Poetry 1913-15*, and its 1915 premiere was a *succès de scandale*, shocking audiences and critics, and remembered as one of the great events of the Georgian years.

In 1914 the Bottomleys moved to the Sheiling in Silverdale. Edward Thomas came in

June, full of excitement about the poetry he had begun to write and his discussions with Robert Frost. He loved the house, 'on a stoney hill all alone, with rabbits on the doorstep', and found a tarn to bathe in before breakfast.[21] The house, with its William Morris wallpapers, was full of beautiful things: pictures by Rossetti, Samuel Palmer, Lucien Pissarro, Edward Calvert and Charles Ricketts. Thomas sent his first poems to Bottomley, who arranged for eighteen them to be published under a pseudonym in *An Annual of New Poetry*, just before Thomas was killed, the first publication of a significant number of his poems. Thomas snatched a few days there again during his brief embarkation leave in 1916. They all felt it was a last meeting. Thomas was now 'a happy and tranquillising presence . . . no longer moody or distracted about the future'.[22] He went for walks with Emily, sat with Gordon, sang the old songs and taught them new, ribald army songs. Together they watched a great storm gather with unearthly colour and light from the Kirkstone Pass and sweep over Morecambe Bay. On the train home next day Thomas wrote 'The Shieling':

> It stands alone
> Up in a land of stone
> All worn like ancient stairs,
> A land of rocks and trees
> Nourished on wind and stone.
>
> And all within
> Long delicate has been;
> By arts and kindliness
> Coloured, sweetened, and warmed
> For many years has been.
>
> Safe resting there
> Men hear in the travelling air
> But music, pictures see
> In the same daily land
> Painted by the wild air . . .

Four months later he was killed at the battle of Arras.

Well Knowe, a gentle, seventeenth century, stone house, had an orchard and well-kept garden, and cuttings and seeds – Bergamot, Larkspur, Old Man, Rosemary – contributed to the Thomases' various gardens. 'Old Man', Thomas's beautiful poem about memory, celebrates the Old Man bush, which continued to move with the Thomas family, a scion of which grows on Edward and Helen Thomas's graves (Thomas's daughter Myfanwy gave a cutting to a Lancaster University postgraduate a few years ago, so it came back to the north-west). Bottomley pictured Thomas at the garden gate at Well Knowe, as he was wont to appear after walking from Grange station[23]:

> Here in the North we speak of you,
> And dream (and wish the dream were true)
> That when the evening has grown late
> You will appear outside our gate –

As though some Gipsy-Scholar yet
Sought this far place that men forget;
Or some tall hero still unknown
Out of the Mabinogion
Were seen at nightfall looking in,
Passing mysteriously to win
His earlier earth, his ancient mind . . .

Ah! pause to-night outside our gate
And enter ere it is too late
To see the garden's deep on deep
And talk a little ere we sleep.

(2) Isaac Rosenberg

Isaac Rosenberg, painter and perhaps the most original of the 'War Poets', was killed in 1918, young, poor and unknown. Probably Bottomley's greatest service to literature was to make sure Rosenberg's poetry was published. His friend Robert Trevelyan showed him some of Rosenberg's poems in 1916, and he sent off two characteristically warm letters: 'His first was all praise and his second all criticism; but his criticism was higher praise than any praise I had been given before',[24] Rosenberg wrote. This was just the period when Bottomley was regarded by many up and coming writers as the epitome of the modern poet, and Rosenberg was a great admirer of his style. 'He was my great god of poetry the moment I read "The End of the World" '.[25] The attractions of Bottomley for Rosenberg are obvious: he was a verse-dramatist using large images with a painter's eye, moving skilfully between blank and free verse, not afraid of grotesque or sexually bold subjects, nor of employing an obscure diction. There is clear indebtedness between Rosenberg's *Moses* and Bottomley's *Sinai* (1907) and *Babel: Gate of God* (1912), though Rosenberg shows an intellectual command, and the gift of developing a complex image through a poem, that Bottomley never achieves. Both had tuberculosis, were outsiders to the London literary establishment, both quarrelled with God in their poetry at times, and both projected psychological states into mythological or cosmic images. 'There never was a more real poet than you . . . I cannot tell you the deep pleasure with which I read *Moses*,' wrote Bottomley.[26]

Rosenberg, suffering as a private in the trenches, continued to write and send out (partly for safekeeping) poems and drafts to Bottomley and other friends. 'Your letters always give me a strange and large pleasure; and I shall never think that I have written poetry in vain, since it has brought me your friendliness . . . Now, feeling as I am, cast away and used up, you don't know what a letter like yours is to me', he wrote in February 1917.[27] Bottomley urged him to write on Jewish themes, and he continued to work at his strange (slightly Bottomleyesque) play *The Unicorn*, as well as the lyrics for which he is now known, until his death. Bottomley devoted much energy to the task of collecting and preserving and deciphering his often fragmentary and near-illegible manuscripts, and was editor of Rosenberg's *Poems* (1922) and co-editor with D. W. Harding of the *Collected Works of Isaac Rosenberg* (1937).

Figure 6.2: Paul Nash, *Foliage*, 1914. View from the back of Bottomley's house in Silverdale.
Reproduced with the permission of The Paul Nash Trust.

(3) Paul Nash and Charles Ricketts

Another young artist to whom Bottomley gave encouragement at a crucial time was Paul
Nash. Nash's model sets for Bottomley's plays *King Lear's Wife* and *Gruach* are his best
stage designs. In 1910 the twenty-one year old Nash was so excited by Bottomley's *The
Crier by Night* that he drew illustrations all over a friend's copy. The friend forwarded
the book to Bottomley, who wrote a letter full of appreciation and advice: the start of a
friendship and correspondence of thirty-six years.[28] Nash's biographer suggests that a
sentence in that first letter profoundly influenced Nash:'the greatest mystery comes by
the greatest definiteness'.[29] Blake, Samuel Palmer and Rossetti had been early inspira-
tions for them both. Nash visited the Bottomleys at Silverdale in 1914 with his fiancée,
Margaret Odeh. 'Their house is a treasure box of books and pictures within, and
surrounded by an enchanted jungle without' (what an apt description of the outsider's
first impression of the low, dense woodland round Silverdale – soon to be increased by
what neighbours saw as Emily Bottomley's mania for planting trees) 'Its windows
command the silver bay and grey hills one way and look east across fine, stumbly,
grey-green country to the Mountains . . . My pictures are promising', he wrote to Eddie
Marsh.[30] Nash painted twenty-seven pictures of Silverdale and the Lake District. Interestingly, his Orchard pictures of his period are in some ways visual equivalents of
Bottomley's Orchard poems: behind both lies a tradition of apple tree and orchard as

101

Figure 6.3: Paul Nash, *The Monkey Tree*, 1914. The tree was in Bottomley's garden.
Reproduced with the permission of The Paul Nash Trust.

symbols of visionary plenitude, as in Calvert and Palmer.[31] Nash's move towards Post-Impressionism and Surrealism after the 1920s caused an intellectual rift, but their friendship remained unaltered. (Figures 6.2 and 6.3)

Bottomley often wrote like a painter *manqué*; some poems were inspired by specific paintings or music; the visual aspects of his books mattered to him, and he was lucky in the friends who designed books or sets for him: Paul Nash, Charles Ricketts, and James Guthrie.

The contemporary artist for whom Bottomley felt warmest admiration was Charles Ricketts (1866 – 1931), printer, painter, sculptor, theatre-designer and jeweller, a person-ality of legendary flamboyance and wit. Ricketts's paintings and Bottomley's paintings often create similar effects: large, apocalyptic images of terror and awe based on ancient legend, dreamlike tableaux of tragic passion. Ricketts, who discovered Japanese art much earlier than other English artists, inspired Bottomley's experiments with Noh drama, and encouraged the use of simple, symbolic stage devices. He was one of the first champions in Britain of the French Symbolists and of Gaugin and Van Gogh. The household he and Charles Shannon created – 'The one house in England where you will never be bored' said Oscar Wilde[32] – was, like the Bottomleys' homes, but more magnificently, a shrine to art: austere bedroom and studio but drawing-and dining-room filled with Persian miniatures, Tanagra figures, Japanese prints and Egyptian antiquities.[33] From Ricketts Bottomley learnt that it was possible, with taste, to become an art collector without being rich. They shared a belief in the primacy of Rossetti, Moreau and the Symbolists as the true sources of modern art, and both were disappointed by the directions Modernism took after the war. They shared also a devotion to Wilde's memory:

> . . . one ill-fated, who loved loveliness
> Unguarded, and lonely died, the sport
> Of treacherous and inhuman men,

in Bottomley's words.[34] Ricketts's last years were darkened by the brain damage Shannon suffered after an accident. Bottomley, like Sturge Moore remained a loyal friend.

(4) Gordon Bottomley: Poems

Turning to Bottomley's own poetry, it has to be admitted straightaway that some of it, particularly from the early years, is terrible: a Pre-Raphaelite nightmare strewn with corpses, drowned nuns, wraiths, and sadistic *belles dames sans merci*. 'The Prey of the Shifting Sands' is typical of the (aptly titled) 1896 collection, *The mickle drede*. It is about death by quicksand:

> It gripped his feet; it gripped his knees;
> It made his bone-pith grue,
> As inch by crawling, slimy inch
> His helpless corpse it drew . . .

The Morecambe Bay area is often recognizable, disguised as Camelot or somewhere more grisly. We see Cartmel Priory with monks, Arnside Tower haunted – as in 'The Lonely Tower':

> It stands on a rising and windy valley,
> A waste diseased and dull . . .

and the Bay itself, the 'Dolorous Bay':

> The sea's thin lip scars a shifting beach
> With a line of leprous foam.
> ('The Prey of the Shifting Sands')

There is a superabundance of *fin de siècle* adjectives like *grave, pale, dim, rose, grey, fading, dread, slim, weary, moon-pale,* etc., and many moonlit orchards. The curiously variegated diction, full of archaisms, coinages and hyphens, is at its worst in *The Gate of Smaragdus* (1904):

> Vine-row on vine-row cluster pied
> Like a feast-progress worship-tied,
> Broidered and hung with filigree,
> Niello, smaragdine tapestry,
> Skim-shadows inlaid daedally . . .

and Bottomley never lost a taste for words like *thrasonical*, *vespertitial*, and *orgulous*. Yet he always had a sharp eye, especially for weather:

> Autumn comes quickly on us hereabout;
> Wreckage of roses strews the garden-ground . . .
>> (*The mickle drede*, 1896)

> When the wind falls the rain falls;
> The air has no more breath.
> The ceaseless 'Hush' of rain
> Is what eternity saith.
> The hills grown near and tall
> Let down a misty mane . . .
> Endlessness weighs on all.
>> ('Night and Morning Songs', 1912)

His poems, though many have fantastical settings – Troy, Renaissance Venice, Babel, or the world of a painting – reflect his immediate environment. The poet's situation is often that of one observing the outward world from bed or window: a reminder of his invalid state, and of his conviction that 'Our own parish is the only place we need when we would find subjects for our art',[35] a passionate certainty that art comes from within and expresses human patterns unchanged by time or place. Thus, remembering his friends, the painters Clinton Balmer and James Hamilton-Hay, working in the Cartmel garden:

> In the lost Valley all is still
> To-day: upon the stony hill
> The heat of the late afternoon
> Settles in coppery haze: and soon
> A voice not known to me will call
> Silent obedient cows to stall . . .
>
> But Well Knowe garden only shines
> In memory now . . .
>
> When James and Clinton harboured nigh
> And working in another art
> Than mine, yet peopled for my heart
> The Valley with the very core
> Of vital beauty for ever more.
>> *Midsummer Eve* (1905)

The early orchard poems:

> From the low open windows we lean down
> And watch the fruit-garth drown
> In the too restful night.
>> 'The Orchard' II

play with contrasts of ripening and falling, and action and contemplation.

He loved the North Lancashire landscape, 'a real landscape with bones in it',[36] and it is reflected in many later poems:

Under the long fell's stony eaves
The ploughman, going up and down,
Ridge after ridge man's tide-mark leaves,
And turns the hard grey soil to brown.
                    'The Ploughman'

O, shepherd out upon the snow,
What lambs are newly born? . . .
I see his long, long shadow go
Across the fields of morn.

Ere dawn the snow-light in the room
Awoke me, and I saw
A pallid earth, a cloudy gloom,
A shape that stirred my awe . . .

He feels not how I watch him creep,
He thinks he is alone;
He searches for the heavy sheep
Each windward hedge of stone.
                    'In January'

Here he turns the theme he had often used, of the natural world observed from a bedroom, into a mature, simple lyric, interweaving contrasts of winter and birth, transience and the moment, individual perception and the cycles of rural work, with an almost Wordsworthian restraint. 'The End of the World' (1907) begins as a precise evocation of a wintry scene and then cuts behind this veil of immediate, sense impression to reveal a permanent and apocalyptic disaster. Employing again the contrast of indoors and out, it opens with a cumulative picture of all-enveloping snow:

The snow had fallen many nights and days;
The sky was come upon the earth at last,
Sifting thinly down as endlessly
As though within the system of blind planets
Something had been forgot or overdriven.
The dawn now seemed neglected in the grey
Where mountains were unbuilt and shadowless trees
Rootlessly paused or hung upon the air.
There was no wind but now and then a sigh
Crossed that dry falling dust and rifted it
Through crevices of slate and door and casement . . .

Gradually we realize that the title is to be read literally:

The coldness seemed more nigh, the coldness deepened
As a sound deepens into silences;
It was of earth and came not by the air;
The earth was cooling and drew down the sky.
The air was crumbling. There was no more sky.
Rails of a broken bed charred in the grate . . .

Though in the description of the snow the world of sights and sounds seems to press particularly closely on the eyes and ears of the watchers in the room, we come to see these phenomena as signs of a cosmic drama being enacted behind them. This effect in the poem is a paradigm of Bottomley's aesthetic creed: beyond the world of appearances is an unseen reality which it is the artist's task to reveal, through symbol, romance or horror. He wrote:

I have spent my own life . . . in remote places whose daily life cannot have changed greatly (except in a few externals) since the time of the Border ballads. My business has seemed to be to look for the essentials of life, the part that does not change. . . Two or three times in forty-five years . . . I have been intently aware of existing in a state not subject to time . . . It can only be heard when stillness transcends itself in motionless activity. In my conception the arts are the language of this immortal state[37]

His geographical isolation, his choice of primitive settings removed from present day 'externals', his confidence in unchanging psychological and artistic truths, his own invalid state and the theme of the immobile watcher, can be seen to be harmonised in this passage, within a single aesthetic.

His most popular poem, the charming 'New Year's Eve, 1913' ('O, Cartmel bells ring soft tonight') expresses longing for Cartmel when far away on Christmas Eve. In 'A Surrey Night' he yearns for the village at night:

I only see my Northern vale
And its steep solitudes;
The hard, lean fells against the night,
Between the darker trees;
The high and distant farm-house light;
The village stillnesses.

'To Iron-Founders and Others' (1908) protests against the foundry at Carnforth. More characteristic is 'The Viaduct' (1906): who but Bottomley would have seen the London train crossing Arnside viaduct as a tragic queen?

And when I found the narrowing estuary
I saw a railway bridge through twilit mist;
It seemed by veils suspended to exist,
But a hushed tide washed under clankingly.

A train from London crossed it in the night:
I woke and saw a tossing burning mane,
And felt some tragic woman passed again
With trailing tresses in dispurposed flight.

(5) Gordon Bottomley: Plays

Bottomley wrote plays from the beginning, and many of his early poems are semi-dramatic. He belonged to that movement (that now seems doomed, despite the participation in it of Eliot and Yeats) to make a new tradition of poetic drama for the twentieth century theatre. The early plays are often embarrassingly bad, but not – as with many fellow verse dramatists, like Stephen Phillips, Masefield, or Sturge Moore – because of a pallidly literary, and over-genteel concept of verse drama, but because of extravagantly over-wrought language and violent, even sado-masochistic themes. These sado-masochistic fantasies have an air of being – but only partly – cliché. He shows an obsession with violent women and with conflict between women, which often goes far beyond a *nineties*-ish preoccupation with *femmes fatales*: these women's power and cruelty operates in areas that extend beyond the sexual arena; it is not merely a projection of male fear. The brutal peasant woman, Thorgerd, in *The Crier by Night*, and the psychopathic Hallgerd in *The Riding to Lithend*, show this motif in its raw state. His obsession with powerful women, with sexual conflict, with forceful relationships between women, and with the psychology of cruelty, developed in his long career as dramatist into something more worthy of respect, and more original. In *King Lear's Wife* (1913) and Gruach (1920), he tells the women's side of two shakespearean tragedies. In *King Lear's Wife* Goneril is the heroine, the loyal daughter to her mother, outraged by her father's infidelities and stupidity, and his neglect of his wife, who lies slowly dying of cancer on the stage. *Grand Guignol* is not absent: the play, with its grisly corpse washers' song, its grim plot and sexual frankness brought Bottomley brief notoriety, and sold many copies of *Georgian Poetry 1913-15*. The most repulsive bits had to be cut from its second production because Lady Tree, who played the queen, 'shrank', as Bottomley put it, 'from too many early British feelings'.[38]

Bottomley's plot is swift and melodramatic, creating a psychological prehistory for Shakespeare's play, and reversing its sympathies. Goneril is a virgin huntress of stark, uncompromised loyalties, just and implacable; Regan is a compulsive eater, and Cordelia a spoilt child hated by her mother: 'Cordeil the useless had to be conceived . . . to keep her father from another women'. The male is a poor creature, as in Shakespeare's play: vain, foolish and lecherous; but here it is only the women who see it to be so, and they have become cynical, grasping and hopeless, for men have power, and even the gods are male.

Gruach tells of the elopement of the young Macbeth and his lady. The future Lady Macbeth is, like Goneril, a Diana-like figure, striding over the moors, rebellious against an unjust guardian, but a spritelier, more sympathetic character. There are several foreshadowings of *Macbeth*, including a sleepwalking scene, but the play lacks the originality of design we see in *King Lear's Wife*, which is almost certainly the first English drama to show *Noh* influence.

Sybil Thorndike played Gruach in London in 1924. Bottomley's plays are striking in their provision of strong female parts: all have more female than male parts; some are wholly female. He offers usually more than one major female character, and although sexual passion and jealousies are important themes, the truly dynamic passions in many of his plays are between women. *The Parting* is a sympathetic study of mother-daughter love, and *The Sisters* shows reconciliation after betrayal.

Bottomley rejoiced in the Celtic and Viking heritage of the North West of England and Scotland. He usually chose ancient settings and ancient, tragic plots, because he believed that elemental human passions were clearest in them. Like Yeats he was trying to achieve in a rebirth of poetic drama a theatre of symbolism, using non-naturalistic staging and designs, rejecting the shallow realism of contemporary, commercial theatre. He was influenced by Maeterlinck, Yeats, by *Noh* theatre, and the theatrical designs of Gordon Craig, Charles Ricketts and the Russian ballet. He became, after 1922, deeply involved in the English and Scottish movements for community and regional theatre.

Undoubtedly his greatest work is in the three collections of plays inspired by Japanese *Noh* drama, published in the 20s and 30s.[38] In some ways he is more successful than Yeats at capturing, and recreating in his own theatrical idiom, something of the spirit that animates the *Noh* with its Buddhist roots. Though his plays are less obviously Japanese in outward characteristics than other Western imitations of *Noh*, they show a deeper understanding of its principles, and it is precisely for that reason that he is able to reinterpret the genre in an original way: creating a type of play which is not imitation but a new development.

Most of the later plays are centred on an ancient story remembered in a particular locality, usually stories from the Scottish religious conflicts of the sixteenth and seventeenth centuries. In these later, choric plays, there is more economy and more humanity than in the early dramas: the macabre and the sensational are still present, but horror and savagery are met by stoicism, and tenderness between the sexes; pity arising after terror. Female characters discover both the strength of courageous endurance, and the resolution that only compassion can bring to entrenched enmities. Women also in some plays touch, in earthly destitution, the borders of mystic discovery. They are plays about time and the infinite, as well as about the local and the universal. Forgiveness solves ancient feuds, and though Bottomley still clearly finds the sexual affinities of cruelty fascinating, there is a wider vision of the complexity of the issue.Indirectly, it is possible to see the plays as, among other things, myths of the emotional dilemmas and traumas of Europe after the devastation of the First World War, even though the plots are usually taken from local legends of a particular parish or community.

He was enthusiastically involved with the Silverdale Village Players. He loved the area, partly because he saw in its landscape and community a continuity with the Celtic and Viking past. He cast a young Silverdale farmer's daughter, Peggy Proctor, with striking fair hair and blue eyes, as the heroine of one of the village plays; in the prologue she says:[40]

> If you should meet me any day
> Outside, you'ld nod and smile and say
> 'That's Margaret Proctor from Knowe Hill'.
> But now I am not she . . .
>
> My name is Vigdis, and you must know
> In Iceland a thousand years ago
> My dwelling is . . .

... the first men who tilled our soil
And built them homes with love and toil
Out of our oaks and dear grey stone
Were Norway men, exiled and lone.

In the dedication to *King Lear's Wife* he had written:

... in my Northern valley I,
Withdrawn from life, watch life go by.
But I have formed within my heart
A state that does not thus depart,
Richer than life ...

... line and sound, colour and phrase
Rebuild in clear, essential ways
The powers behind the veil of sense;
While tragic things are made intense
By passion brooding on old dread.

Despite the mystical terms in which he wrote and thought about literature, the elemental patterns that his writing reveals are emotional ones. His work dramatises obsessions and probes psychological tensions. He was an arch-Romantic; he did best with large images and a broad brush; his artistic judgement was always rather hit-and-miss; he often could not distinguish between a bold effect and an absurdity. Yet he had great imaginative verve, and at times he could write very well. His plays have been virtually ignored, but there is much that is original and much that, particularly in a feminist era, deserves new attention. Young Arthur Ransome had caricatured Bottomley as a bankclerk intoxicated with poetry, and there is a lot of truth in the caricature, but something more central is captured in Edward Thomas's picture, of a cold northern habitation which has been made

By arts and kindliness
Coloured, sweetened, and warmed.

Notes

I would like to thank Miss M. Pennell of Silverdale for much interesting information about Gordon and Emily Bottomley in Silverdale.

1. Edward and Helen Thomas stayed with Bottomley in April, 1904; Ransome visited Bottomley soon afterwards, staying with his cousins in Cartmel: Arthur Ransome, *The Autobiography of Arthur Ransome*, ed. Rupert Hart-Davis (London, 1976), pp. 90–1.

2. From an unpublished account of his life, quoted in Gordon Bottomley, *Poems and Plays*, ed. Claude Colleer Abbott (London, 1953), Introduction, p. 10. *Poems and Plays* contains many of the works mentioned in this paper.

3. *Letters from Edward Thomas to Gordon Bottomley*, ed. R. George Thomas (London, 1968), p. 4.
   See also R. George Thomas, *Edward Thomas: a Portrait* (London, 1985), esp. 103, 122–29, 250. Bottomley introduced Thomas to Guthrie.

4. Thomas, *Letters*, p. 55.

5. Ransome, *Autobiography*, pp. 99–100.

6. *Ibid.*, pp. 90–1.
7. *Ibid.*, pp. 96–7.
8. Arthur Ransome, *Bohemia in London* (London, 1907), pp. 128–9.
9. *Ibid.*, p. 129.
10. Arthur Ransome, *The Souls in the Streets* (London, 1904), pp. 37–44.
11. Ransome, *Autobiography*, p. 108.
12. *Ibid*, p. 129. Generally on these visits see *ibid.*, pp. 110–12, 128–30, and Hugh Brogan, *The Life of Arthur Ransome* (London, 1984), pp. 47–9.
13. Thomas, *Letters*, pp. 40–1.
14. Review in *Daily Chronicle*, 5th December, 1902.
15. Ransome, *Autobiography*, p. 110.
16. Gordon Bottomley, 'A Note on Edward Thomas', *Welsh Review* IV (September, 1945), 71–4. 17. Thomas, *Letters*, p. 76.
18. *Ibid.*, p. 57; see also pp. 86, 186, 206; and Brogan, p. 36.
19. *Ibid.*, p. 57, pp. 89–90.
20. Helen Thomas, *As It Was, and World Without End* second edition (London, 1972), p. 159.
21. Eleanor Farjeon, *Edward Thomas: the Last Four Years* (London, 1958), p. 75.
22. Bottomley, 'A Note', pp. 177–8.
23. *Ibid.*, pp. 168–71. See the Dedication to *The Riding to Lithend*, in *Poems and Plays*, pp. 94–5.
24. Isaac Rosenberg, *The Collected Works of Isaac Rosenberg*, ed. Ian Parsons (London, 1979), p. 249.
25. *Ibid.*, p. 238.
26. Joseph Cohen, *Journey to the Trenches: the Life of Isaac Rosenberg, 1890–1918, (London, 1975)*, p. 150–1.
27. Rosenberg, p. 252.
28. See *Poet and Painter: being the correspondence between Gordon Bottomley and Paul Nash, 1910–1946*, ed. Claude Colleer Abbott and Anthony Bertram (London, 1955). This was reprinted by the Redcliffe Press (Bristol, 1990), with an introduction by Andrew Causey. 29. Anthony Bertram, *Paul Nash: the Portrait of an Artist* (London, 1969), p. 80; *Poet and Painter*, p. 3: Bottomley insists on the importance of skill with 'outward appearances' for the artist of 'inward ideas'.
30. *Ibid.*, 77.
31. Andrew Causey, *Paul Nash* (Oxford, 1980), pp. 52–6, for Silverdale and Lake District pictures; pp. 56–9 and 352, note 73, for the Orchard pictures; p. 40 on the theme of female power in Nash, Bottomley and Thomas. See also Paul Nash, 'Outline', in Bertram, *Nash*, esp. 160–162, on Bottomley.
32. *Self–Portrait: taken from the Letters and Journals of Charles Ricketts, R.A.*, ed. T. Sturge Moore and Cecil Lewis (London, 1939), p. 16.
33. See Jacques-Emile Blanche, *Portraits of a Lifetime* (London, 1937), pp. 130–3; *Self-Portrait*, pp. viii–x; Stephen Calloway, *Charles Ricketts: subtle and fantastic decorator* (London, 1979), pp. 6–24; Joseph Darracott, *All for Art: the Shannon and Ricketts collection*, Fitzwilliam Museum, Cambridge (Cambridge, 1974). 34. Lines cut out from the 'Dedication to C[harles]. H. S[hannon]. and C[harles]. S. R[icketts].', prefixed to *Gruach*; see letter from Bottomley to Shannon and Ricketts, 16th December, 1921, Kendal Records Office. On his distress and illness after the Wilde trial, see *Self-Portrait*, pp. 298–99.
35. *Poet and Painter*, p. 46.
36. *Ibid.*, p. 63.
37. *Poems and Plays*, p. 12.
38. Quoted in Robert H. Ross, *The Georgian Revolt: the Rise and Fall of a Poetic Ideal* (London, 1967), p. 153 (note). On G.B's drama generally see Kenneth Muir, 'The Plays of Gordon Bottomley', *Essays and Studies*, New Series, XXXIII (1980), 139–153.
39. *Scenes and Plays* (London, 1929); *Lyric Plays* (London, 1932); *Choric Plays* (London, 1939). See also Helen Phillips, 'Gordon Bottomley and the Scottish Noh Play', in *English Studies, III: Proceedings of the Third Conference on the Literature of Region and Nation*, ed. J. J. Simon and Alain Sinner, Publications du Centre Universitaire de Luxembourg (Luxembourg, 1991), pp. 214–33.
40. 'Prologue for the Silverdale Village Players to *The Locked Chest*, by John Masefield, Easter 1924', *Poems and Plays*, pp. 78–9.

Contributors

David Craig was born in Aberdeen; he has a daughter and three sons. He is married to the writer Anne Spillard and lives in Cumbria, in eyeshot of Dow Crag, the Old Man of Coniston, and the Langdale Pikes, and his most recent books are *On the Crofter's Trail* (Cape), *King Cameron* (Carcanet), and *The Grasshopper's Burden* (Littlewood Arc).

Keith Hanley was born in Bolton and, after graduating at Oxford, he lectured for several years in Sweden and West Germany. At present he lives with his Polish wife and two children in Lancaster, where he is a Lecturer in English and directs the Wordsworth Centre at the university. He has edited critical editions of nineteenth-century poets, collections of essays on Romanticism, revolution and editing, and is the author of many articles, including some on Wordsworth and Ruskin.

Alison Milbank studied for her doctorate in the English department at Lancaster University, and held an honorary fellowship in the Wordsworth Centre. She is now the John Rylands Research Institute Fellow at the University of Manchester. Her *Daughters of the House: Modes of the Gothic in Victorian Fiction* is to be published this year by Macmillan.

Helen Phillips, who was born in Newcastle-under-Lyme, is a lecturer in the English Studies Department at the University of Nottingham. She previously lectured at Lancaster University and lived in Lancaster for fifteen years. Her publications are mostly in medieval literature, but they include a recent article on 'Gordon Bottomley and the Scottish *Noh* Play'.

David Steel was born in a West Riding mill-village, and educated at home, Bradford Grammar School and Magdalen College, Oxford, before going to teaching posts at the École Normale Supérieure and the Sorbonne in Paris. In the Department of Modern Languages at Lancaster University, where he is Senior Lecturer, he combines research in modern French and German writing and painting with an interest in local literary history. In 1979 he mounted and wrote the catalogue for the Lancaster Museum exhibition on *Laurence Binyon and Lancaster*.

Occasional Papers from the Centre for North-West Regional Studies

Flowering Plants and Ferns of Cumbria	G. Halliday	£2.95
Early Lancaster Friends	M. Mullet	£2.95
Traditional Houses of the Fylde	R. Watson/M. McClintock	£2.95
North-West Theses and Dissertations, 1950–78	U. Lawler	£6.00
Lancaster: The Evolution of its Townscape to 1800	S. Penney	£2.95
Richard Marsden and the Preston Chartists, 1837–48	J. King	£2.95
The Grand Theatre, Lancaster	A. Betjemann	£2.95
Popular Leisure and the Music Hall in 19th-century Bolton	R. Poole	£2.95
Industrial Archaeology of the Lune Valley	J. Price	£2.95
The Diary of William Fisher of Barrow, 1811–59	W. Rollinson/B. Harrison	£2.95
Rural Life in South-West Lancashire, 1840–1914	A. Mutch	£3.95
Grand Fashionable Nights: Kendal Theatre, 1575–1985	M. Eddershaw	£3.95
The Roman Fort and Town of Lancaster	D. Shotter/A. White	£4.95
Windermere in the nineteenth century	O. M. Westall	£4.95
A Traditional Grocer: T. D. Smith's of Lancaster	M. Winstanley	£4.95
Reginald Farrer: Dalesman, Planthunter, Gardener	J. Illingworth/J. Routh	£4.95
Walking Roman Roads in Bowland	P. Graystone	£4.95
The Royal Albert: Chronicles of an Era	J. Alston	£4.95

Each of these titles may be ordered by post from:

**C.N.W.R.S.,
Fylde College,
University of Lancaster,
Bailrigg, Lancaster**

**Books will be despatched post free to UK addresees.
Please make cheques payable to 'The University of Lancaster'.
Titles are also available from all good booksellers within the region.**